CHANGE IN THE FARM

CHANGE IN THE FARM

BY

T. HENNELL

With illustrations by the Author

CAMBRIDGE
AT THE UNIVERSITY PRESS
1936

CAMBRIDGE UNIVERSITY PRESS
Cambridge, New York, Melbourne, Madrid, Cape Town,
Singapore, São Paulo, Delhi, Tokyo, Mexico City

Cambridge University Press
The Edinburgh Building, Cambridge CB2 8RU, UK

Published in the United States of America by Cambridge University Press, New York

www.cambridge.org
Information on this title: www.cambridge.org/9781107651401

First published 1934
Second edition 1936

First paperback edition 2011

A catalogue record for this publication is available from the British Library

ISBN 978-1-107-65140-1 Paperback

CONTENTS

ILLUSTRATIONS

PREFACE

IN every farmyard, outhouse and contingent building throughout the country are to be seen—piled-up relics of past generations of farmers—the remains of old ploughs, waggons and implements crumbling away behind the new steam-thresher and brightly-painted iron rakes and harrows.

The following compilation is an attempt to collect and arrange some of this lumber, whose wormy and twisted forms with their crust of fowl-dung may prevent their uses from being discerned, though upon closer scrutiny their character becomes recognisable. They are warped and rubbed down to the accustomed knots and sinews of the hands of their ancient proprietors, and so reveal themselves as emblems of family history. But what exactly were their names and uses, and what the just and time-honoured methods of those who wielded them, are not in a moment to be recognised; they are to be extracted only at leisure from a welter of daily commonplaces, the genial warmth of fire and beer bringing them ripely from the dwindling memories of the third generation back. An account of them may be not unlike that of Bunyan's man with the muck-rake, eternally collecting scraps of straw and wood; but all the country's history, and not only a chronicle of small-beer, is written out in the carpentry of broken carts and waggons, on the knots and joints of old orchard-trees, among the tattered ribs of decaying barns, and in the buried ancestral furrows and courses which can still be traced under the turf when the sun falls slantwise across the fields in long autumn afternoons. There are many old ways of sheafing, tying knots and so forth, which were familiar enough a generation or two ago, but are now mysteries among the ancients and little cared for by the practical, unprosperous young farmers of to-day.

The following is an attempt at an orderly arrangement of such methods, so condensed as to be readable by those who have loved the land without following the plough— by no means to be commended as a piece of writing nor yet exactly as a practical treatise, except in so far as politicians may read history as a guide to modern reforms. When farmers have laid aside the formidable engines, hooks and harrows of modern agrarian reform, they may return like Cincinnatus to their fireside turnips and consider how things were done when tools were simple and the land was fed upon straw-yard muck.

T. H.

November, 1933

NOTE TO THE SECOND EDITION

As a new edition of this book is found to be practicable, the public which was mainly so indulgent to the first is here offered still more material at much less cost. More solid writing the author would like to have added, and to have avoided some trivial and contentious points. But it was agreed to keep the print as it stood, only adding supplementary pictures, in the belief that the first-hand record was worth more than artificial composition. Again such thanks as can thus be expressed are offered to farmers and others for occasional hospitality, ungrudging help and pure goodwill. The thanks of the author and publisher are due to the Council of the Newcomen Society for permission to reproduce the illustrations on p. 17 and the straw doll and page of straw ornaments among the added drawings at the end.

T. H.

Ridley, *August 1936*

CHANGE IN THE FARM

Chapter I

THE FARMHOUSE

BY way of beginning a book whose purpose is to record some still-existing aspects of traditional English husbandry, it has seemed to me that a plain picture or inventory of a farmhouse of the old sort may be the most natural centre and starting-point of the divers activities of its household.

The house which I have chosen is a large one, of solid proportions and regular features, with wide passages and fairly spacious rooms; with a healthy atmosphere, especially in the back quarters, of clean whitewash and scrubbed brick. In front there is a walled enclosure, containing a grass plot, fringed with laurels, yews, holly, box, bay, and other evergreens which somewhat shade the corners of the house; with an aloe or monkey-puzzle on the green. Under the windows are one or two flower-beds, bordered with moss-grown scollops and other marine prodigies, but though not altogether neglected or untidy, these plots hardly show evidence of constant care and attention. There is a straight formal walk from the iron front gate to the square front porch, the stone doorstep and heavy green front door, with knocker, bell and ornamental knob. But the whole house-front has a somewhat conventional and forlorn air, as if it exists for the sake of respectability rather than for use and pleasure. Indeed this entrance is not the one which is generally used; so we had perhaps better go round to the back.

Here it is seen that the house is planned as three sides of a hollow square, enclosing a flagged yard, in which the many farm cats are daily fed. In the central part of the house and one side the farmer and his family live, the other wing being reserved for the unmarried labourers, who have a separate stairway to their sleeping-quarters above the scullery and kitchen. The kitchen is the largest and most comfortable room in the house, and on Sundays and holidays, when left to themselves, the family take possession of it for meals. It has a brick floor, lime-washed walls, and plain wooden table, chairs, cupboards, flour-bin and dresser; the last furnished with enough blue and white crockery to serve a regiment. The kitchen-clock and a frame worked by pulleys from the ceiling, to dry clothes before the fire, complete the essential furniture. The oven-range is enormous; on it, beside the food of the household, are cooked the potatoes and meal for the poultry, pigs and calves.

A good deal of space is occupied by rooms subsidiary to the kitchen. A step down leads out into the scullery—on whose stone floor, beside the pump and sink, pails and buckets tend to accumulate—and thence to the larder, pantry and wash-house. The adjoining buildings, once the bake-house and brew-house, are now made to serve for storing coals and poultry-meal. The dairy is across the yard; a cool place close to the main water-supply—a stream which passes by the house and is used to turn a small wheel to work the churn. Besides this latter there is a butter-table, and the walls are lined with shelves and trestle-tables, covered with an array of separating-pans, crocks and other necessary utensils.

From the dairy the passage leads to the office, a room hung with prize-certificates of bygone agricultural shows, and with files of discoloured papers suspended from the ceiling; containing among other things a bureau and safe, a bookshelf filled with ledgers and back numbers of farming magazines, a calendar advertising cattle-food or embrocation, one or two guns and some stuffed rarity in the way of fur or feather. This room is often used by the family for breakfast or tea.

The dining-room proper is reserved for occasions of more elaborate ceremony; it is dark and dignified, with a heavy table and chairs, a grandfather clock, and a massive sideboard covered with never-used articles of plate. The ceiling has a moulded border, and the walls are hung with a paper whose surface of solemn red is broken by several large pictures: one or two family portraits and some maple-framed engravings—"Highland Cattle" and "Queen Victoria Opening Parliament".

The parlour is the room in which occasional visitors are entertained and in which the family assembles in the evenings. Its decorations are of a lighter sort—daguerreotypes of patriarchal wedding-groups and pictures of favourite horses or prize beasts. This is the one room besides the kitchen which generally has a good fire in the winter, and for this reason it is secretly used by the mistress as an airing-room for the family's linen.

There is a drawing-room also, but this, it must be owned, is the coldest and least frequented room in the house. It has a piano, some water-colour views which suggest needlework, vases, a fire-screen, and such furniture as is too delicate or infirm to endure the strain of everyday use.

It may be added that a wide passage at the back of the house connects the office and kitchen. To the wall at one side, above a row of boots, is fixed a range of long wooden pegs, with facetted bosses; together with the usual collection of hats, great-coats and the like, these support several bridles, saddles and other pieces of riding-harness used by the master and regarded as being of too good quality to be hung with the rest in the harness-room by the stable.

Of the upstair rooms it may be enough to remark that they include a large linen-cupboard, a store-room and an apple-room; and that the bedrooms are irreproachably clean and comfortable.

THE OUTBUILDINGS

Behind the house, but not immediately contiguous to it, is a large oblong stockyard, fenced with stakes, and separated by a cobbled space from the surrounding out-buildings. These may be briefly catalogued here; more will be said of their particular uses hereafter.

Close to the back-door, and partly screening it from the yard, is the granary, a square building mounted on staddle-stones, of timber-framed construction and with a pyramidical tiled roof. Next, in a row along one side, come the wood-shed, store-houses, cider-house and work-shop—the last was once a forge. Another side is given over to cow-houses, stalls, and loose-boxes; above which are hay-lofts and a space for the turnip-slicer and cake-crusher. Here are the piggeries, a long series of covered sties and walled enclosures. The barn fills the whole end; it is an immense structure of oak beams, some of which may have served centuries ago as part of ships or barges, braced together and fastened with trenails and covered with a patchwork of tarred weather-boarding. The foundations are of brick and flintwork, crumbling in places, but still quite capable of bearing the enormous weight; most of which, indeed, is carried by the brick piers which support the main upright posts inside, at a distance of a dozen feet within the outer walls. Resting upon these are horizontal beams, the transverse ones carrying king-posts, on which again are timbers running lengthwise from end to end of the barn, crossed by short tie-beams, one to each pair of rafters. The thatch is sewn on to laths, or split rods, nailed across the rafters; the upper layers being pegged upon the first ones. The ingenuity of the barn-builder is very strikingly shown in his management of corners and setting-out of gables, which are very simply contrived without weakening any part of the whole. But the expense of thatching has of late years caused the roof to be somewhat neglected, and the rafters now begin to stick out bare in one or two places, like ribs through the hide of a dead horse.

Beside the barn are the stables, in a separate building, and the road runs past these through the rickyard, and thence out into the fields. There are other buildings by the rickyard: cart-houses, the fowl-house and other sheds, and under a clump of elders the now disused saw-pit—somewhat like a brick-lined grave—with the remains of a thatched shelter. There is also at one end of the barn an old broken-down "horse-works" with cast-iron gearing, by which the threshing-machine and chaff-cutter were formerly operated. A couple of rick-stands support the wheat-ricks, and there are also several haystacks, a cut clover-stack smelling of the very best tobacco, and a purple-brown stack of bean-haulm. Odd corners of the yard are taken up with old carts, ploughs and harrows, which on account either of their decrepitude or of their evidently imperishable nature are not thought worth while to house under cover. By the gate is the hull of an antique waggon, half-buried like a wreck on a sandbank, sinking into a bed of nettles and rubbish.

Chapter II

COWMAN AND DAIRY

THE farmer or cowman gets up at about half-past four in the summer, or six o'clock in the winter, and calls in the cows for milking. They are turned out immediately after and are milked again, as a rule, about four in the afternoon. Near Frome, in fine weather, the cows are milked in the fields; and I have heard that this is done in some other places.

The cow-house or shippen, if it is of the old sort, is a long building which has a stone cobbled floor with a gutter down the middle and stalls with pairs of upright posts along either side, between which the cows are tethered. But these stone floors will not be seen much longer, for by Act of Parliament farmers must put down floors of concrete instead. On the sweet breath of the cows, the steady sound of crunching and the hiss of the milk into the pails, it is unnecessary to enlarge; no doubt the old style of hand-milking will be practised for many years to come, though the mechanical milker is used on very many farms, and though less pleasant to the imagination it is, one is told, not less acceptable to the cows.

By increased production price is often reduced, and thus things are made more difficult for the small producer. One farmer complained that a government instructor had taught him and his neighbours to get three gallons of milk a day where they formerly only got two; the result was that while feeding cost more they got no more money for their three gallons than formerly for two, the demand not having increased with the supply. "Now if he had taught us to get only one gallon", he concluded, "there would only be enough milk for those that want it, and we should get a better profit than we do now!"

The large farmer is naturally inclined to consider his animals not as individuals, but as mere units of efficiency; but it is by no means so with those who have only a few, upon which their living depends. The poor people in Kerry used to give the cow the first place before the hearth in their cabins; they kept them indoors not, as Arthur Young suggested, to save the manure, but because the warmth increased their yield. An Irish shepherd keeps his lambs, too, in the house at night, "to save them", as he says, "from the dogs".

Few people have any idea of the extent to which domestic animals respond to personal care, nor what intimate understanding of them is possessed by those whose lives are passed in tending them. To illustrate this I copy out the following note, made last year:

"F. S. was anxious about a mare which was going to have a foal, and she dreamt one night that it had two foals, one a fine red fellow with three white legs and a white nose, and the other one a little tiny thing no bigger than a dog. There came a great black dog and carried off the big fine fellow and left the little one. The next morning she went out and there the two foals were, at the very spot in the Barn Meadow, between the ditch and the apple-tree by the gate, exactly as she had dreamed of them, a big one and a little one. They reared the little one with a bottle, and it lived and was afterwards sold, but the big one fell sick and died after a fortnight. At many other times F. has dreamed of things which have happened, especially with animals she was rearing."

Dairywork has come to belong to factories instead of, as formerly, to the farmer's household: the whole day's milk being more often than not put through coolers and taken off in a lorry. But the old processes of skimming

off the cream, churning, salting, and rolling the butter
are too well-known to justify an account here.

The separator has taken the place of the brass and
earthenware pans or lead coolers, except in Devonshire
and Cornwall, where clotted cream is made in the old
way, by scalding over the fire. Several forms of churn
are made; nowadays they are nearly always of the
"barrel" or "end-over-end" types. The old upright or
dash-churns, in which the work was done by means of a
plunger, bored with holes and with a long handle, were
made in the northern counties by some coopers who are
still in business; but though a few of them are no doubt
in existence still, they are long out of fashion and have
been replaced by more modern types. As everyone
knows, a cool hand is an indispensable qualification of a
good dairymaid, for pressing the buttermilk out of the
butter, without making it heavy or greasy. In the north
of Dartmoor this was not long ago a still more important
gift: for the cream was put in a tub and churned *by hand*,
the dairywoman's arm being plunged to the elbow. In
the Science Museum at South Kensington there is a most
elaborate engine for turning a barrel-churn by gears from
an immense spur-wheel, the power having been supplied
by a horse or bull.

Whatever may be the popular notion in the matter,
good farm-butter is better in colour, richer and more
nourishing than factory butter; indeed it *tastes* of butter,
which the hard, white stuff sold by grocers does not. It
does not pay a farmer to "blend" or adulterate his
butter, but to make it of as good quality as possible.
Butter like flour, bread and meat, is devitalised and its
wholesome nature destroyed, the more it is passed
through mechanical processes.

A substitute has in the same way been found for farmhouse cheese, in the form of a tough gelatinous matter wrapped in tinfoil; which, though it costs the customer as much, is more profitable to the shopkeeper. However, in spite of this competition, some of the better sorts have survived, while in Suffolk one may be fortunate enough to get excellent cream-cheese, in place of the once famous flinty substance described by Bloomfield, made from "three-times skimmed sky-blue", which, after defying all attempts to cut it with a knife, at last

"in the hog-trough rests in perfect spite,
Too big to swallow, and too hard to bite".

Nowadays essence of rennet, for curdling the milk, is bought from the grocer, but the old way was to salt and dry the maws or vells of sucking-calves and to keep them for a year before use, then making an infusion from them in water or whey, with the addition of lemon-juice. Occasionally a decoction of the flower called "yellow lady's-bedstraw" was used as a substitute for rennet.

Cheeses of different kinds are produced partly by differences of pasture or feeding, but chiefly by the different states of the milk, or milk and cream, at the time of curdling: several "meals" of milk being some-times combined, the night's cream, for example, being added to the morning's whole milk. The curds were first separated from the whey by cloths and then packed into cheese-tubs or chessarts, the cheese-press being used to squeeze out the last of the whey. But the old wooden cheese-presses, with stones weighing a couple of hundred-weight, and the clumsy screw-presses which succeeded them are long since done away with, and the whey is now pressed out of the cheese by a more simple and efficient system of weights and levers.

"Green cheeses" used to be coloured in Wiltshire

with sage, marigold and parsley leaves, bruised and steeped overnight in milk; the leaves being sometimes left in the cheese. "Double Gloucester", an excellent cheese, was painted outside, after salting and scraping, with a mixture of Indian red, or Spanish brown, and small beer; it was known by the "blue coat" which in time appeared through the paint. Egg-cheeses were made in the north of England, three or four yolks going to every pound of curd.

THE SHEPHERD

Fashions have changed in shepherding as in all other branches of farming, more especially perhaps in things outwardly noticeable. The shepherd's smock has disappeared almost completely, even from Sussex, the last county in which that splendid and serviceable garment continued to be worn without shame. There were decided differences in the styles of smock which prevailed in Sussex, Suffolk and Dorset—doubtless in other counties also—and much diversity of ornament in each. The shepherd's was a long smock, reaching below the knees; the carter's came only to the thighs.

There is, it seems, less variety among modern than ancient shapes of sheep-crooks; and some at least have ceased to be made. Several blacksmiths, however, specialise in them and each has his own pattern. There is a famous maker of crooks at Pyecombe in Sussex, who is said to have made them for several bishops. The narrow part of the opening of a crook is reckoned to be just wide enough to pass the first thumb-joint, which in a shepherd's hand is inclined to be larger than in another's.

Sheep-bells are heard on the Sussex Downs, where the difficulty of locating the flocks otherwise, among the hills and hollows, makes them indeed a necessity. There are a few flocks with bells in some other counties—in Berkshire, Cambridgeshire and Gloucestershire—but they are becoming something of a rarity. The old sort, called tankard- or canister-bells, which were carried on a light wooden yoke with a couple of leather thongs, have sometimes been replaced by round latten-bells, which in past years belonged to horse-teams.

The shepherd's calling may seem at first sight a leisurely one compared with that of a ploughman or other labourer, but it is by no means so in fact. He is generally the most independent of the farmer's servants, because the most responsible. Quite apart from his anxieties and sleepless nights at lambing-time, his daily work, as of folding—that is, moving and setting up hurdles in a field in which sheep are being fed—is heavier than most labourers will willingly undertake.

Some time between Christmas and the end of March is the shepherd's harvest; and for a few weeks he must be constantly watching and attending to the sheep, day and night. Given fair weather, the lambs will do better in the open than under cover, but if any should be born outside on a frosty night, when the shepherd is asleep, he may come in the morning to find them dead and frozen to the ground.

If a ewe loses her lamb, she will generally act as foster-mother to the second of a pair of twins; though, until it has assimilated her milk, she will not take kindly to a strange lamb. To make her do so more readily, the new lamb is often "coated" or covered with the skin of her dead one. But I have heard an experienced shepherd, with a very thorough understanding of animals, declare that this old custom is unnecessary and that it is enough if he stands by the pen in which the lamb and foster-mother are first introduced and watches them quietly for the first ten minutes or so. She will make no attempt to attack or reject it in his presence, and thereafter all will be well.

When the mother dies, or there are triplets, and a lamb is left unprovided for, with no ewe to take it, it is often brought up by hand and fed from a bottle—such lambs are in some places called "cosset-lambs".

Different breeds of sheep need very different degrees of care. The Welsh and Scotch mountain sheep are much more hardy than the lowland breeds; they will pick up a living for themselves with very little winter-feeding. The lowland sheep must be fed well and housed in severe weather, and must be more carefully guarded against disease. It may be of interest to mention one or two old remedies. Stockholm tar is used for foot-rot and to protect sores; warm milk for liver-fluke; blue-stone or copper for the fly, which lays its eggs in any cut or sore place in the sheep's skin and whose maggots feed upon and putrefy the flesh. An old Gloucestershire farmer carries about with him from June till September a copper penny of George III, in the efficacy of which he has entire faith. "They can't stand copper," he affirmed, "he'll shine avore the zummer's out!"

But since prevention is better than cure, the sheep are "dipped" in a solution which renders them immune to the fly, soon after they are shorn. Nowadays they are as a rule lowered in a sort of cage like part of a pair of scales; but the old dipping-troughs are made of stout planks, with a sloped draining-board on which they must stand for a moment after clambering out, to let as much as possible of the precious liquid run back. A tool made of a strip of hoop-iron with two wooden handles was used to hold them under; they must be submerged in the dip all but their heads, for they must not swallow any.

Sheep-shearing takes place generally in June, and many farmers have a fixed date on which they like to begin the work each year. The sheep are washed about a fortnight before this time, though of late years many farmers have abandoned the practice, as not repaying the labour, for washed wool fetches but a halfpenny a pound more than unwashed and the loss of weight makes the difference yet slighter. The last consideration is the reason why some time is allowed to elapse between washing and shearing: so that the "yolk" or natural grease, which forms an appreciable part of the weight of the wool, may return into the fleece. Sheep are washed in a stream if there is one at hand; and it takes four men to wash them: two standing in the water and swaying them from side to side, while two more take them from the pen.

There are several styles of sheep-shearing; and since the old-fashioned hand-shears are sooner or later likely to give place altogether to machine-shears of one kind or another, some account of hand-shearing may not be amiss here.

In Kent, where there is still plenty of hand-shearing done, there are two distinct styles, known as the "Marsh" fashion, which is followed in Romney Marsh, and the "Uphill" style, which is in general use elsewhere. The Uphill shearers begin at the belly and work straight upwards, coming down the head, back and sides and finishing with the hindquarters. The Marsh shearers, on the other hand, start with the head and take first one side and then the other, clipping round the belly instead of up it. The latter method is sometimes preferred on the ground that it lessens the risk of losing sheep from "twisted gut", a rather obscure mischance, seemingly the bursting of a blood-vessel, which sometimes befalls them during shearing, especially during hot weather and after much handling.

The shearer first catches his sheep in the pen by one hind leg and, drawing it backwards to the cloth on which it is to be shorn, throws it on its side by a vigorous jerk and then stoops over it to begin. As he does the head and side he stands, raising the sheep on its haunches and bending over it; as he goes down the back he holds its head between his knees; when he finishes the tail and hind legs, he kneels over it, holding its head down by placing one foot athwart its neck. As a rule the sheep submits with a fairly good grace and seems to be caused but little inconvenience by the operation, but a ram is more disposed to be refractory and two men are sometimes needed to hold him quiet. The fleece is taken off all in one piece; and the shearer, catching it up at one shoulder, first winds a rope of this on his hand and then, tucking in the sides and end and packing in it any loose locks or "fly-wool", rolls it up like a blanket, securing it with the twisted end, drawn firmly round the bundle and turned under itself. On an old ewe, the wool may be matted and coarse and lacking in that springiness which is natural to good wool, so that it is difficult to tie up; such a fleece is called a "cott" and is worth less than the regular price.

Sheep-shearing can only be done satisfactorily in fine weather, for to cut well the fleece must be dry. It is easy to tell a sheep which has been shorn by hand, and even the style of the shearer; for each cut of the shears is visible, so that the newly-shorn sheep appears as though carved with bold, definite strokes of a chisel or adze out of some crisp white material. But a sheep which has been shorn by machinery is of a more uniform surface, and its coat instead of being spongy to the touch seems

Sheep-shearing at Berwick Hill Farm, Lympne, July 6, 1931

hard and "boardy". Some farmers greatly prefer hand-shearing, partly for the better appearance of condition which it gives to yearling lambs and partly because, as some maintain, "the wool grows better after the shears than after the machine".

At any rate, there is no pleasanter rural sight than a band of shearers at work under the shade of trees on a fine day in June. A farmer who has only a few sheep may undertake the shearing himself, or with one man's assistance, but in important sheep-districts there are bands of shearers who go round every year and do the work with admirable speed and dexterity. From the end of May to the second week in July they are at it daily, moving from one farm to the next with their shears and sharpeners; and at the end of the last day they throw up their hats as a sign that the season's work is ended and return to their regular jobs till the following summer. This throwing-up of the cap is a last vestige of a custom in use at the old sheep-shearing festivals, at which an empty drinking-horn was thrown into the air in the cap and caught as it came down. Some sheep-shearing songs, such as "Old Job", exist still in the memories of the older farmers and labourers here and there, but with the decline of the old ritual they are remembered only in a casual, fragmentary way and seldom or never sung.

A mention, at least, must be made here of sheep-dogs, the indispensable allies of shepherds; and it may be noted that they are as often of the collie as of the rough-coated kind. Frequently the dogs are clipped at the same time as the sheep, and very unsightly objects it makes them for the time being, however much it may increase their comfort in the sultry part of an English summer. Of their cleverness and sagacity nothing need be added, nor of the celebrated sheep-dog trials which are annually held in the Lake District and elsewhere. A peculiar survival in Westmorland may, however, be finally noticed, and that is the remnant of an old Celtic language, which is, or was lately, used for counting sheep. In Borrowdale the numerals one to twenty are as follows:

1–5. Yan, tyan, tethera, methera, pimp.
6–10. Sethera, lethera, hovera, dovera, dick.
11–15. Yan-a-dick, tyan-a-dick, tethera-dick, methera-dick, bumfit.
16–20. Yan-a-bumfit, tyan-a-bumfit, tethera-bumfit, methera-bumfit, giggot.

The Wasdale form is this:

1–5. Yan, tian, tudder, anudder, mimph, etc.

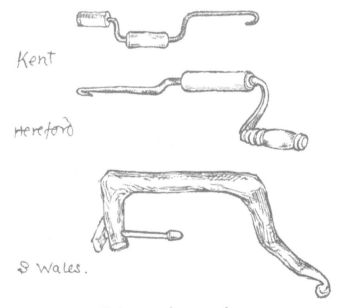

Kent

Hereford

S Wales.

Twiners or throw crooks

Chapter III

THE CARTER AND THE STABLE

HORSES have not ceased to be the most valuable servants of many farmers, and so the carter's duties need not be very elaborately particularised here. In the morning he must clean and groom the horses and "set the stable fair", he must feed and look after them during the day, and late in the evening "make up for the night". The cleaner the stable is kept the better, and the fresher the horses will be; but some carters have strange notions about this. There is an old idea to the effect that if the cobwebs, which in some stables hang like dingy stalactites from the rafters, are swept away, the horses will catch cold.

In old stables there is an oak corn-bin or "ark", with divisions for bran and oats, and a wooden peck measure. It seems difficult now to get the large black oats which were such a valuable part of the horses' food. Carters of the old sort would sooner starve themselves than their teams and by some farmers were given a bad name for pilfering corn to pamper them. For drinking, horses prefer soft water to hard, though now they often get the latter, since most farms have the Company's water "laid on". Some country places, however, are still dependent on ponds for their supplies and when these go dry in a hot summer the farmer may have to send his water-cart for miles. A Kentish farmer complained that when the rain came again the horses would not go back to the pond-water and so he had to "bring them to it gradual", by adding a little muddy water every day to the clean.

The chaff-cutting machine consists generally of a wheel with curved blades fixed to the spokes, which cut the hay as it is automatically fed through a trough; it can be worked by hand, but where any considerable quantity is wanted it is driven by a horse-works or a small engine. This form of chaff-cutter has been known since 1800 or earlier, but a more primitive kind is occasionally seen, though practically never at work. This, in Kent, was called a "monkey-box". To use it one had

Chaff-cutting machine (Shalbourne, Berks)

to push the hay along the trough with a short fork held in the left hand, to compress it by treading upon a lever with the left foot, and to cut the chaff by a sawing movement of a knife hinged on another lever. It seems an extraordinarily cumbersome invention, but it was actually quite speedy and efficient in an accustomed hand.

Where the horses' tails are allowed to grow long, they are sometimes plaited with straws and ribbons, and to do this well is no fool's job. Both carters and farmers

2-2

have often decided views as to how exactly it should be done. The old loose hairs are pulled from time to time and fresh ones take their place. An old farmer near Rhayader made all the rope which was used on his farm with the pullings of the horses' tails, and most extraordinarily tough rope it must have been.

Carters are less employed now as such, for with the increase of motor transport road-waggons are no longer used for long journeys, except in a few flat parts of the country—in Cambridgeshire, Lincolnshire and parts of Kent and Sussex. But wherever horses are kept for ploughing and other farm work, there is a man whose job is to look after them; sometimes, though not so often as formerly, a head carter with a second and third under him. When the waggon was taken on the roads, the carter walked beside on the "near side" in his smock and with his breeches tied up with whipcord, carrying his whip with its brass-ringed handle and accompanied by a boy or under-carter, for an assistant was necessary to adjust the skidpan or "drag-shoe" on hills, or perhaps where other traffic was encountered. Often a journey had to be made to the mill with a load of corn to be ground, perhaps at a distance of five or six miles, and for this the carter had to be up at two in the morning, in order to be back in time for the regular day's work. Five quarters was about the capacity of a Kent or Sussex waggon, and the journey had to be made once a week. Sometimes the distance was more considerable; in parts of Wales lime was carted for fifteen miles, and elsewhere farmers sent to towns over twenty miles distant for "night-soil" or even farther to attend markets or buy cattle. From the latter it might not be necessary to be back so early, but they might have to start at midnight in order to be there in good time in the morning. In making these expeditions the carter would wake himself at the right hour, and though he had nothing but the stars to tell him the time the position of the Plough would tell him exactly when he must set out.

It was the carter's duty to keep an eye on the waggon and point out necessary repairs before it was too late, and also to see to the state of the shoes and harness. Some farms of middling size kept a forge and a man who could act as farrier, but except on large estates this is very rare now. The occupation of carter was often hereditary, and the horse-bells and brasses were handed down from father to son.

HORSE-TEAMS, BELLS AND BRASSES

At fairs and festivals the waggons as well as the horses were often decorated; the former with ears of corn tied in bunches to the lades and ladders, the latter with bells and brasses, and their manes and tails "ridged.up" or braided with straw and ribbons. It was no rare thing for the carter to be up by four o'clock on a week-day morning, or late on Sunday night, polishing the brasses in preparation for such an event or simply because the team was to be taken out on the roads the next day.

The ornaments, as has been said, are as a rule the carter's property. There are large and small horse-bells. The former, called latten-bells, are of the size of hand-bells, three or four to each horse, the set making up a full, rich scale. They are fixed to the hames by a hooped rod, and being protected at top and sides by leathern flaps studded with small brass plates are known also as box-bells. Their old use was to warn on-coming traffic at night or in narrow winding lanes where it was difficult for meeting vehicles to back; they are to be found in the southern and western counties more than in the north.

The small bells, fastened on an upright ornament on the horses' heads or singly at the sides, make a constant slight tinkling or all jingle suddenly whenever a horse shakes his head. These are the head-bells; and though latten-bells are hardly ever to be seen in use at present, small bells and brasses are kept by a good many carters who take a pride in their teams—fewer now, it must be owned, in the country than in London and other large towns.

Sometimes a swinger takes the place of the head-bells, a small round plate of polished brass suspended in a brass ring, which glitters like a mirror as it swings. But what are generally called the "brasses", or amulets, are irregular plates or discs about three inches across, in the form of some device, fastened either singly at the forehead or in a series to the broad piece of leather between the collar and the girth-strap, known as the martingale or breast-strap. These ornaments are said by antiquarians to be of very ancient origin; some supposing them to be referred to in the Bible (Judges viii. 21, 26), others considering them to have been charms against the evil eye. Among the commonest forms are the sun, moon and stars; the lotus and ox's head, and many trefoil and other shapes derived therefrom; roses, thistles, wheels, knots, trees, horsemen, horses, beasts, cocks, windmills, monograms and crests. There are brass studs and sometimes larger ornaments such as hearts, diamonds or stars, on the hame rein, and brass plates of more or less richness on the loin straps (which are purely fancy additions to the harness) and sometimes on the blinkers, though these used often to be embossed with raised or moulded shapes worked in leather—cockle-shells and such like. The edges of these pieces, and of the box-bells' covering, were often ornamentally incised or stitched.

For the comfort of those amateurs who collect horse-amulets, it may be added that these are still cast, at Wolverhampton, from old moulds and sold by saddlers in several parts of the country; as also are some inferior stamped brasses of later invention and others inset with knobs of coloured porcelain. Besides these, small head-bells, swingers and coloured brushes or plumes may be had new, but not many young horsemen will afford five shillings for these extravagances, although, it may be remarked, they can quite often pay for a seat at the cinema.

"Pride in horses! why, that's a thing o' the past."

BULLOCK-TEAMS

In early times oxen were almost universally employed for ploughing, heavy horses, the ancestors of our shire-horses, being fewer, it is supposed, than at present and being kept as chargers for the use of the nobility.

In 1760, as Young records, bullocks were still about as commonly used as horses on the farms of England. After this time, with the improvement in the breeds of horses and the general introduction of lighter ploughs which could be drawn by two horses, the old teams of eight or twelve oxen were generally abandoned, though in a few districts, such as the Sussex and Berkshire Downs and in parts of Wiltshire and Gloucestershire, they continued to be in fairly common if not general use.

In Sussex many farms kept a score of oxen and used them for drawing carts on the roads, as well as for work on the land. Such carts are still sometimes to be seen; they were adaptable to shafts for a horse or to a pole, called a neb, which could be fixed to the yoke by which the two oxen drew it. When taken on the roads it was necessary to have them shod; the shoes consisting of two plates, one for each part of the hoof, sometimes with a flange inwards. The cost of shoeing was a halfpenny for each shoe—that is fourpence for each beast. Many of these bullocks were sent from Wales to Sussex and to London; and as they travelled by road a smith accompanied them to mend or replace shoes which had been broken or lost on the journey. The same thing was done when Aberdeen Angus cattle were sent to London, a distance of three hundred miles, which they accomplished by road in three weeks.

Up to 1914 there were a dozen or more teams at work on the Sussex farms; by 1931 there were none, the last team belonging to Major Harding at East Dean having been given up in 1929. But it is not impossible that their use might be revived if arable farming should again become profitable in that district, for they are said to suit the land better than horses. They have several advantages: though slower than horses, they pull with a steadier draught, they are cheaper to feed, they are much less nervous, and will work close under hedges and in places where horses will not go. They would sometimes bolt, plough and all, when "terrified" by flies; but to prevent this a dressing can be easily and effectually applied. When they had been worked for ten or a dozen years (they are three or four years old when they begin), they were fattened for beef, which was sold in Sussex at fourpence a pound.

The only team left in England in 1931 was the celebrated one of six Hereford cattle which belonged to Earl Bathurst at Cirencester. These Herefords are in constant work between 8 a.m. and 4 p.m. and yet are always fat and well-looking. At seven o'clock in the morning, before starting, they are fed with hay, which

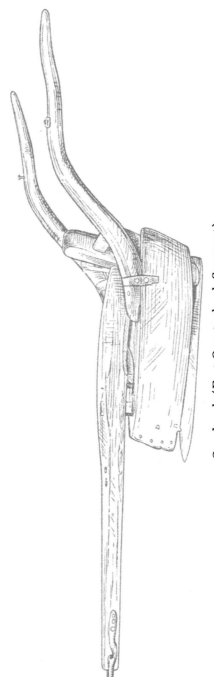

Ox-plough (East Quantoxhead, Somerset)

will stay by them for the rest of the working day. At half-past eight or nine, on reaching the ploughland, they rest for a while, and again at midday, when they ruminate their hay; at four o'clock they are watered and then turned out to grass and need no more attention until the next morning. During one day they can plough an acre of ground with a double-furrow plough, with no unusual exertion.

This team and others that were lately used in Gloucester-shire are not harnessed with yokes, but collars; a practice which has been adopted by Rhodesian farmers. Instead of bits to the bridles the mullens, as they are called, have a chain under the jaw and a rein on the left-hand side only; to turn them to the right a verbal command must be given. The hames and cart-saddles are made of wood, as light as possible. The harness becomes very soft and supple with use, from the natural grease of the oxen; not dry and cracking as with horses.

Many farmers in Devon and other counties hang up in their halls the ox-yokes which were used in their grandfathers' times; these are generally made of oak carefully carved into shape and often blackened and polished. The "bows" by which they were fixed to the necks of the oxen were made of ash, steamed and bent into shape and passed through two holes in each curve of the yoke.

The primitive-looking ox-plough which is illustrated was used within the memory of its present owner's father. The ox-man had three or four songs, which he sang continually over and over again; and when he stopped singing, the oxen stood still in their tracks.

WAGGONS AND CARTS

"Horse, oxen, plough, tumbrel, cart, waggon and waine,
The lighter and stronger, the greater they gain:
The soile and the seed, with the sheafe and the purse,
The lighter in substance, for profit the worse."

THOMAS TUSSER.

To make waggons as light and strong as possible was and is the great concern of country wheelwrights. This practical object is the primary reason for most of the chamfered ornament on the older types, for no superfluous ounce of weight must be left, and the joints and corners must therefore be thicker and stouter than the intermediate parts and those on which the strain is slight. Oak is the timber most used for the framework of the waggon, elm planks for the sides and floor, elm logs for the naves of the wheels, ash for the spokes and fellies and also for the shafts.

It is scarcely an exaggeration to say that there is a different style of waggon to each county; for though certain of the old types are to be found in several counties and are not restricted to a single one, there was some distinctive peculiarity in the work of almost every individual waggon-builder in the country. The harvest- and road-waggons are the central types of the old county patterns, but besides these there are among the older sorts timber-waggons, millers' and brewers' waggons, and many other varieties; double-shafted and pole-waggons, hermaphrodites, bavin-trucks, flat bed-waggons; and many species of two-wheeled carts, tumbrils, butts and the like. Apart from the work which is now done by lorries and engines, the old types have in many districts given place to what are called trollies and boat-waggons, and in many more the traditional county pattern is altered and debased and shorn of all curious elaboration.

Four-wheeled waggons are named according to the amount of turning which is possible to the front wheels: quarter-lock, in which the movement of the wheels is limited by the straight sides of the waggon-floor; half-lock, in which a section is taken out of each side, forming a "waist" in which the wheels can turn further; three-quarter lock, in which only the pole of the waggon impedes their movement; and full-lock waggons, in which the wheels are made small and can turn under the floor of the waggon. The last sort are generally made now, their front wheels being about three feet high; but formerly all four wheels had to be large, so that the axles might clear the ground when the waggon went in the ruts, which in many country roads were, within the last fifty years, nearly two feet deep.

The differences between the traditional types can be realised better from illustrations than from description. It is a striking fact that some parts of the country are fifty years or more behind the fashion elsewhere; for example, straked wheels, which have been abandoned for many years in North-east Somerset, are still made sometimes in the south-west part of the county; and they are also used in parts of Sussex, Kent, Essex, Suffolk and Hereford. In Radnorshire one may even see wooden-armed axles made still, though in most parts of the country iron arms have been in use for the past seventy years or even longer.

The waggons of the eastern counties differ from those of the western, in having as a rule a straight pole, instead of a curved one, to join the front and back axles. Some of the former have also a chain on either side, from axle to axle, to limit the movement of the wheels as well as

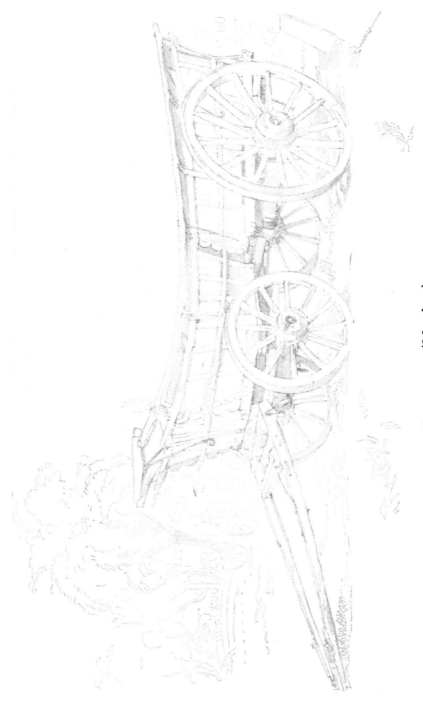

Kent waggon (Meopham)

Hereford waggon (Mathon, nr Malvern)

to share the strain on the waggon-pole when turning a corner. The lades, or raves, at either side, are in some patterns curved continuously from end to end; in others they are divided into two parts, a convex curve over the hind wheel and a concave curve over the front one, by which means the floor could be made lower and the stability increased.

Hermaphrodite waggons, known in the vernacular as "mophrodites" or "mufferers", are used largely in North Lincolnshire and about the Norfolk Broads. Originally these were made simply by taking the shafts off an ordinary two-wheeled cart, fixing the front wheels of an old waggon to it by means of a simple framework, and adding a long overhanging "copse" or front lade. Now the front wheels and attachment are specially made, though the hind part can be used for the ordinary purposes of a two-wheeled cart. They are quite light and easy to turn and will hold almost as great a load of hay or straw as an ordinary waggon, and therefore are very convenient things for harvesting.

In Oxfordshire and Buckinghamshire another improved form of waggon is used, the Woodstock waggon, which was developed in the latter half of the eighteenth century. It is lighter and handsomer than most of the old patterns; the side lades, tail and front boards being barred instead of boarded and the former symmetrically curved over the hind wheels.

The Gloucestershire "hoop-raved" waggon represents one of the older types; the one illustrated was built over a century ago and was used for carrying hay until 1929. The inside of it is an oblong rectangle, with rather high sides, quite upright—in most other waggons they are sloped somewhat outwards—and the floor quite flat. The wheels run several inches further apart than in some of the other types; the axles are of wood throughout and very massive. The arms on which the wheels turn taper from six inches in diameter to three; the outer end is surrounded by an iron ring and several stout nails are beaten in to make it hold fast. Behind this ring is the linch-pin, secured from falling out of place by a "chog" of wood keyed into the stock (as the nave of a wheel is called here) and there fastened by a latch. These stocks are very massive and the spokes are set into them in mortises which come all to one level, instead of being alternately advanced and set back, as in the smaller stocks which modern cart-wheels have. The wheels are straked, each strake covering the junction of two fellies. The tail-board has two claws beneath, fitting into staples in the shutlock (the hindmost floor-timber), and by means of a chain at either side it can be lowered outwards to any degree. There are no detachable lades or harvest-ladders —"gates", as they are called in Gloucestershire, were more lately introduced—and it needed much skill and judgment to load up and balance the load without them. Such a waggon as this requires much space to turn in— not less than a quarter of an acre of ground. The front wheels can only move a little way before they scrape the sides of the waggon-floor; and if a carter tried to turn too quickly, he might easily upset the load or, if the wheel were an old one, the end of a strake might catch against the iron and so break the wheel to pieces.

Though it is not as a rule difficult to tell to what part of the country a given waggon belongs, what may be called a thoroughbred county pattern is not always to be found, for the style of building has sometimes changed considerably in the past century or so, not to speak of more modern changes. So in Northamptonshire, for instance, there are several old kinds, differing as much

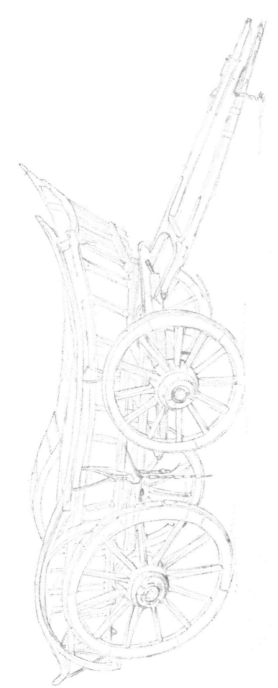

Gloucestershire "hoop-raved" waggon (West Littleton)

Norfolk type of waggon (Lutton, Lincs.)

from one another as from most of those which are to be found in Norfolk, Suffolk, Essex, Bedfordshire and Hertfordshire.

There is, however, in several counties a local tradition of painting. In Lincolnshire great pride is taken in the waggons, which are very handsome, and the carts too are often elaborately carved and decorated, the farmers saying that "it pays to keep them painted up". The name of the painter, as well as that of the owner, is often put on waggons when they are redecorated; the lettering being picked out and flourished in black upon a background of orange, which fades in time to terra-cotta. This colour is used also in Cambridgeshire—and not only for waggons, tumbrils and cole-seed carts, but even for ladders, wheel-barrows and dog-kennels—though some very old waggons, it is said, were painted blue, as in many other counties. In Yorkshire the waggons are mostly of plainer design, though some of the road-waggons are much more elaborate than those which are intended for rough work. In the West Riding pole-waggons are common, instead of those with shafts, and many different colours are used to adorn them: red, orange, lead-colour, blue and white, brown or black; and in place of curves and flourishes, "stringing and lining" in a second colour is usual. Kent waggons are often painted cream or stone-colour, Woodstock waggons an ochreous brown; elsewhere they are usually blue above, with red for the wheels and under-carriage, but in Dorset blue-black is sometimes used instead of blue, picked out with red on all the curved chamfers.

The carter walked on the "near" or left side of the waggon, and on that side for his convenience were hung the drag-shoe and drop-chain in hilly counties, to fix the hind and front wheels respectively when going down-hill.

Sometimes two men and a boy accompanied a four- or
five-horse team. In Kent and Sussex there is sometimes
a little box in front, called the waggon-box, which contains the waggoner's dinner. A full-sized Kent waggon
will hold one hundred trusses of straw, that is one and
a half tons. This load is roped on either side, and the
ropes are fixed to the hooks at each side of the waggon,
turned round the end of the lade, and passing over the
load are pulled through the holes in the roller at the tail
of the waggon and drawn tight by means of levers in it.
The cost of such a waggon before the war was about
£28, and it took some months for a village wheelwright
to build.

In Yorkshire and Lincolnshire the waggons will carry
from three to three and a half tons of corn, in Rutland-
shire as much as four tons; while ten quarters of wheat
was the regular load for the old Norfolk and Suffolk
waggons.

As has been said, few such waggons are made now, or
have been for many years, in most parts of the country;
but many of those that exist are likely to last for another
fifty or sixty years, except where their use may become
definitely uneconomical. No pains were spared by the old
blacksmiths and wheelwrights who put them together,
and it is no easy job to knock one to pieces.

As it is, however, there are many counties in which
old waggons are rare and some which have practically
none. In hilly parts of the country, and where there are
sunk and winding lanes, as in Cornwall and Devon,
heavy four-wheeled waggons are little used. The older
Cornish waggons are light and small; and full-lock
waggons were common in that very progressive county
before they had come into general use elsewhere. In
several mountainous districts, slides or sledges alone

were used for carrying hay or turf, and on Dartmoor till 1850 or 1860 W-shaped panniers or half-round dung-pots, slung on horseback, were the sole conveyances for heavier matters. In Radnorshire there is still used a very curious compromise between a waggon and a sledge, called a gambo or ground-cart, which has two large wheels and two heavy bosses or slides at the tail, so that it can be drawn up-hill on the wheels and can come down-hill like a sledge, with the wheels locked. The adjoining counties of Cardigan and Montgomery have their own county patterns of waggons.

There are nearly as many varieties of two-wheeled farm-carts as of four-wheeled, different shapes being used in many districts; but to describe these in detail would take too long. With the improvements in roads the heavier types, with six-inch wheels, are being given up in favour of lighter ones, and many which were made for peculiar purposes, such as the very deep seed-carts, earth- or marl-carts, water-carts, and bob-wheels, are no longer made, their purposes being answered by more modern vehicles.

"Hermaphrodite" waggon (Horncastle, Lincs)

Chapter IV

HEDGES AND DITCHES

BEFORE the Enclosure Acts were passed, somewhat more than a century ago, by which the
common-field system was abolished in most parts
of the country, people often had narrow strips of land in
a dozen or more different parts of a parish; but by these
Acts the separate holdings of each individual were united.
In consequence, a man who had the right of grazing a
cow and a few geese on a large common, could no longer
support them on a small parcel of ground which should
represent his grazing right. This was done in a way which
was very convenient to the larger landowners, but deprived
the poorer people of many of their ancient privileges.

In the old common-field system, by which the arable
land was sown with wheat for two years in succession
and left fallow for the third, the furrows were generally
winding, in the form of a long inverted S. These winding
furrows are to be seen at the present day in a few parts
where the old system still exists. Their form is generally
explained to have been caused by the need for ample
turning space at the headlands, when teams of eight oxen
were commonly used. The headlands were rights of way
to all the inhabitants of the village; and after the enclosures it was usual to make lanes of them, planting a
new thorn hedge on the other side of the way. Though
the individual plants of these hedges may not in many
cases be the original ones, yet their character remains
much the same; and so, in many districts, the hedges can
be clearly divided into two classes:

(1) The old ones, made of holly, nut, elder, maple,
etc., and generally winding.

(2) The new ones, made at the time of the Enclosure

Acts, all of thorn, and, except where they follow along-side the old ones, straight.

This was made clear to me by Canon Marcon of Edge-field Rectory, Norfolk, who has traced on an old tithe-map the original positions of the common lands and the changes made by the enclosures of 1815.

The bank, hedge, and holl or ditch, must all be main-tained by the owner of the land on the side towards the bank. Such hedges as this, when they become overgrown, are partly cut down to a height of about eighteen inches and partly cut half-through and laid down or pleached, the pleaches being pegged down to the bank with wooden crooks, made from those stems which are quite removed. The upright stems which are left are sometimes called "live keepers".

In most parts of East Anglia, however, hedging was done in a very rough and ready fashion; in Suffolk and Essex it was usually thought sufficient periodically to hack the plants down to a height of three or four feet. But here, as in other counties which had no proper tradi-tion of their own, the county organisers, whose duty it is to provide agricultural education, have introduced the more thorough and scientific methods of the Midland counties. In this way the Leicestershire style has been introduced into West Suffolk and the Northamptonshire style into Shropshire; so that, while many rustic arts have declined, in this one there have been some advances, though, to confess the whole truth, many farmers in Leicestershire, Northamptonshire and other counties have of late years grubbed their hedges to save the expense of keeping them cut and laid.

A brief account of the Leicestershire practice will serve as a specimen of the ways of pleaching or laying a hedge. To begin with, the bottom of the hedge and the ditch (if there is one) are ridded, or cleared of all dead wood and such growth as is in the way and cannot be used. Then the smaller and less conveniently growing pieces are cut clean off (half a dozen yards, perhaps, being taken at a time), and the stouter and longer stems are notched rather more than half-way through, laid over, and the projecting part of the notch cut off with an upward blow of the axe. The last-mentioned detail is omitted by most hedgers, but it does much to prevent the stubs from rotting. The pleaches are laid over all in the same direction and stakes are driven in so as to come alternately behind and in front of the stems laid over, but the ends of the pleaches are made to finish all on one side, that is to say, on the opposite side of the hedge to the notches. At first these stakes are driven in about a yard from one another, but as they become filled up with successive pleaches, other stakes are driven in, till at last there is little more than a foot between them. As has been mentioned, the hedge is laid in short sections and when two sections have reached this stage, the first is "eddered" or "heathered". The hedger treads down his pleaches so as to make a firm and solid hedge and winds round the tops of the stakes long, clean rods of hazel, laying the first rod or "edder" with its butt-end behind the first stake and the next one with its butt on the other side of the second stake; and so on successively and alternately, the edders being twisted round each other to form as it were a double-stranded rope, with the heads of the stakes coming at intervals between the strands. As he finishes this, he tightens the edders and drives in the stakes still more firmly with blows from the back of his axe. It only remains to collect the brushwood into heaps and burn it, and, if necessary, to dig out the ditch and make up the bank.

It is not necessary to particularise the other ways of laying a hedge; they may vary according to whether the hedge is made against sheep, which would push through below, or cattle and horses, which would break it down at the top. It may be laid with the ends of the pleaches all to one side, as just described, or with them finishing on alternate sides, so that both sides of the hedge look alike. Where the latter plan is carried out, the plants will probably be set not in a single row, but in a zigzag, so that the stems may cross when they are laid.

A hedge may be grown on other foundations than the Norfolk "bank and holl". It may be planted on a ledge which is left between the ditch and the bank of earth dug out from it; or else a shallow ditch may be made on either side and the thorn-plants set by a line along the mound between. Where a new piece of hedge is planted on an old bank, a new bank, small and neat, is sometimes made along the top of the old one. The old name for the mound on which the hedge grows is the floor-bank, or flower-bank; a hedge without one, consisting simply of a row of quick with a railing on either side to defend it till it can defend itself, is called a foot-hedge.

The old hedgers, when they laid a hedge, used often to lay a wreath of brushwood along the bottom as a sort of foundation for it; but though it might look neat enough at the time, it was a very bad preparation, for it would rot and spoil the bottom of the hedge.

There is, however, another kind of hedge-making in Huntingdonshire, called dead-hedging; fences, that is, are made from stakes interwoven with "writh" or brushwood, and finished with edders, in the ordinary way of laying a hedge. The hedges are very well made in a few districts and last surprisingly long considering their materials, though writers of a century and more ago condemned them as being wasteful and extravagant.

The hedger's first need is a stout pair of gloves; the old sort are made of white-leather—that is to say, pickled horse-hide—and have two divisions only, one for the thumb and one for the fingers. He will probably also have a pair of leather knee-pads, especially when laying a hedge. For this work his tools are an axe and a bill-hook. If the plants are young the axe will not be necessary; the notches are made with the bill-hook and the stakes driven in with a mallet. Hedges are generally laid in January, February or March.

It is hardly necessary to describe the autumn work of hedge-cutting, which is done on tall hedges with a long-handled slash-hook and on short ones with a hedging-bill. With the latter a wooden crook is most often used, though the Sussex hedgers use a small wooden rake. It is most important to slash upwards so as to leave a clean cut; if the tool is brought down on it, the hedge will be badly broken and damaged. The top must be cut well back so as not to overshadow the bottom. A good hedger does not keep topping young plants, though he cuts back the side branches, so that the wood in the middle of the hedge may form a strong natural fence. Some hedgers cut back a hedge against cattle on one side only at a time; and the rough side of a cow-hedge was called a beaver.

The right way to stop a gap in a hedge is to pull several branches across, fixing them there with pegs, and if necessary driving in two or three stakes to protect them. But it is more common to see a dead thorn-bush pulled into the hole, which prevents the surrounding growth from filling it; an old bedstead-rail or worn-out implement is a better makeshift.

In parts of Wales, and elsewhere, the thorns are

allowed to grow up at intervals for an ornament; and when these little trees are about a couple of feet above the hedge, their twigs are often twisted together so that they may grow into a compact ball. In Kent hollies are similarly left to grow up at intervals, though they are allowed to grow freely by hedgers of the older school, and they are a most cheerful ornament. Another Kentish practice is to plant lines of prune-damson or bullace trees between fields, less for a fence than to break the wind and on account of the fruit which these very hardy trees produce; and round hop-gardens quick-hedges are grown sometimes to a height of fifteen feet, to serve as a screen from the wind. In many places also shaws or hedge-brows were allowed to extend on one side of a hedge; and these supplied much of the fuel which was burnt in every farmhouse.

Whitethorn is no doubt the best sort of hedge for all purposes; blackthorn is slower-growing, but will grow on wet cold soil. Crab-apple was anciently used much and was very good indeed, though as a hedge it is almost unknown now. Beech-hedges are the best for plantations, for they keep their dry leaves all the winter, breaking the force of the wind. Holly is too slow-growing to be much used except round gardens or here and there in hedges of mixed kinds. Yew, when dead, is poisonous to cattle and must be kept out. Elm, hazel, dogwood and maple are quite good, but elder, ash and willows should not be allowed; they choke the neighbouring growth in the summer and leave the hedge full of gaps in the winter. Ground-ivy, brambles and briars are also bad for hedges, though the latter are well enough where they grow along the top of a walled mound, especially if they are cut back every year.

The trees which were most generally planted in hedgerows for timber and appearance are elms; next to these oaks and ash. Elms are generally cut back to the trunk for fifteen or twenty feet from the ground, so as not to shade it unduly; and in Middlesex and North Kent they used to be lopped almost to the top, which left them looking like a row of mops. In many counties beeches are set in long avenues or groves beside the roads, but they ought not to overhang cultivated ground, for nothing will grow beneath them.

DRAINAGE

No farmer can farm successfully against water; if his fields are in a water-logged state his labour and manure are thrown away. The initial expenses of drainage are very heavy; pipe-draining costs £10 an acre or more and few will undertake it in a time of agricultural depression. Land drainage in England was raised to the level of an exact science by Elkington in the latter part of the eighteenth century and his methods are the basis of modern practice; so in a book such as this it is not necessary to discuss more than a few details connected with it.

Broadly speaking there are four types of land which may need to be drained; that in which an underlying layer of rock prevents the water from soaking away or holds it stagnant; boggy land; stiff clay, which becomes saturated with rain in wet weather and will allow no more to soak through; and land which is below the level of the sea and rivers. The drainage of the last-named is of course a public undertaking and outside the scope of the individual farmer. Rocky ground is drained by cutting trenches down to the surface of the stone obliquely across the direction in which the land slopes, thus leading away the water to the nearest stream. In some cases where there is stagnant water under a layer of rock, holes are drilled with a four-inch auger at intervals along the bed of the trench. The clay and mixed lands are those for which a greater variety of remedies have been invented, and some of these may be described.

Heavy clay land may crack in a hot summer to a depth of four or even six feet, but in the winter it will absorb water and swell until it can hold no more. If tile- or pipe-drains are laid, they are sunk to a depth of 2 ft. 6 in., though some of the old ones are considerably deeper. The old tile-drains in Cambridgeshire consist of two parts, a flat tile below and a horseshoe-shaped one to cover it, and they are arranged to follow the downward slope of the surface. The modern pipes are narrower and round. A still older way of making drains was to dig a wedge-shaped trench, about thirty inches deep, a foot wide at the top, and two inches at the bottom. The trench was dug in successive spits, with a set of long and tapering land-ditching spades of several sizes. Finally, the bottom of the ditch was made clean and smooth with a narrow scoop, curved back towards its handle. Brush-wood or thorns and straw were trodden in, so that only the bottom of the trench would be clear for the water to flow along, and the trench then filled in again. A better way was to make a "shouldered" trench with a ledge above the bottom on which the brushwood could rest. The first eight or nine inches of depth of the trench were often made by ploughing backwards and forwards with a double-breasted plough, thus saving part of the expense of digging.

As it was only necessary to make a passage in which water could run freely, the bottoms of trenches were often filled with flints, faggots, bones, or any other material through which the water could run, provided that the clay above were heavy and sticky enough not to fall in and choke its course. Indeed there still are drains in the heavy clays of Essex which were simply made by filling the bottom of the ditch with straw rope, and they have lasted long after the straw has rotted away.

This must have suggested an invention of the end of the eighteenth century, the mole-plough, which, in a very greatly improved form, is still the cheapest and most effective means of draining heavy soils. The modern mole-plough is drawn across the field by a tractor; it consists of a steel beam or framework which rests upon the surface of the ground, having a disc coulter in front, to make a deep cut in the soil, and behind this a narrow blade, going to a depth of sixteen or eighteen inches and ending in a solid pointed bar or torpedo, which is thus dragged along underground, leaving behind it a continuous burrow in the clay. The point of it is turned downwards, so that it does not work upwards, as it would otherwise tend to do. These drains often last for many years and have a certain advantage over pipe drains in that instead of being liable to be choked, their sides being of clay are continually scoured by the water which flows through them.

When these machines were first made, they were extremely cumbersome wooden engines; sometimes drawn by a chain and winch, which was securely anchored while its handles were turned by eight women, or sometimes drawn by horses. One such plough, to drain at twenty-two inches depth, was made to be drawn by twenty horses, harnessed five abreast! But it was soon realised that mole-draining is effective at a much slighter depth and with a mole of little more than an inch in calibre. These alterations, with the invention of the disc coulter, very greatly lightened the work, and old mole-ploughs (or "clunch-ploughs", as they were sometimes called in Cambridgeshire) are occasionally to be seen which could work effectively with four horses. I have seen one which was made by a village blacksmith, but the blade and mole were too thick and clumsy for it to do its work well.

MANURING: PARING AND BURNING: MARLING

MARL, CHALK, FLINT-PICKING, PARING AND BURNING, OLD-FASHIONED ANIMAL MANURES, ARTIFICIAL MANURE.

There is hardly a farmer of the old school who does not swear by "muck" and hold artificial manures in abomination. The opinion generally expressed is that chemical manures act as stimulants, producing better crops the first year, but leaving the ground exhausted, so that it is necessary to go on using them in the following years, and that all the time the land is getting poorer and more wretched. Some exceptions are occasionally made; it is generally admitted, for example, that basic slag has lasting effects on a pasture that is not too wet, yet there are many farmers who will hesitate to use this. The greatly increased cost of labour, however, makes it impossible for every small farmer to keep a stockyard throughout the winter, as used formerly to be done, and so the cattle are often allowed to wander about the meadows, doing no more good, as one farmer put it, "than if they was walking about over your garden".

The old farmers did not by any means depend entirely upon animal manure, though they used it in larger quantities than is possible to many now, and a much larger proportion of their crops, being fed on the farm, returned much of their goodness to the land. It was realised that the amount of straw which a farm produces does not make enough manure to prevent the land's fertility from decreasing, and various materials were put on the land to make up for the loss: marl, chalk, ashes, and many kinds of organic manure.

In Norfolk, Suffolk, and the Weald of Kent marling was a regular and most important business. In the Norfolk four-year course, of wheat, turnips, barley or oats, and grass or clover, the land was marled every fourth year, after the hay; half as much marl as manure being used. This was found to strengthen the straw of the wheat, so that it could withstand the July storms; the yield also would be greater and of better quality. It is often complained now that English wheat is too soft to be of much use to the miller, while that which is grown on many farms is full of small withered grains which are almost worthless. The use of marl in Norfolk is now exceptional, though a few farmers who can afford the initial cost of digging, carting and spreading, still find it worth while. There were tumbrils built on purpose to carry the marl, and Norfolk and Suffolk are full of disused marl-pits.

In the same way, Kent and Hertfordshire are full of old chalk-pits and chalk-holes, for the most part without any trace of a lime-kiln, for till lately chalk in its crude state was carted on to the fields, and indeed there are some farmers who use it still, and on grass its effects are evident and lasting. It was spread once every ten years. In other places shells (in their natural state, ground, or calcined), crag (a shelly gravel), and sand have long been and still are used.

Rodwell's account of marling and chalking is quoted by Arthur Young in his *Farmer's Calendar*, and as he describes exactly how it was done some extracts may be made here:

"Clay is much to be preferred to marle on these sandy soils, some of which are loose, poor, and even a black sand. By clay is to be understood a grey clayey loam, some of it brick earth, and all has with vinegar a small effervescence. Marle is a white, greasy, chalky substance, that effervesces strongly with acids: I make a universal rule, on a second improvement to lay clay on the fields marled before, sometimes marle where clay was spread before, but this not general, as clay answers best on the whole".... "The method pursued in Hertfordshire in chalking land is this; and the persons employed therein follow it as a trade: a spot is fixed upon, nearly centrical to about six acres of land to be chalked. Here a pit about four feet in diameter, is sunk to the chalk, if found within twenty feet from the surface; if not, the chalkers consider that they are on an earth pillar; fill up the pit, and sink in fresh places, till their labour is attended with better success. The pit from the surface to the chalk, is kept from falling in by a sort of basket-work, made with hazel or willow rods and brushwood, cut green, and manufactured with the small boughs and leaves remaining thereon, to make the basket-work the closer. The earth and chalk is raised from the pit by a jack-rowl on a frame, generally of a very simple and rude construction. To one end of the rowl is fixed a cart-wheel, which answers the double purpose of a fly and a stop. An inch-rope of sufficient length is wound round the rowl: to one end of which is affixed a weight, which nearly counter-balances the empty bucket fastened to the other end. This apology for an axis *in peritrochio*, two wheel-barrows, a spade, a shovel, and a pick-axe, are all the necessary implements in trade of a company of chalkers, generally three in number. The pit-man digs the chalk and fills the basket, and his companions alternately wind it up, and wheel its contents upon the land:

when the basket is wound up to the top of the pit, to stop its descent till emptied, the point of a wooden peg, of sufficient length and strength is thrust by the perpendicular spoke in the wheel into a hole made in the adjoining upright or standard of the frame, to receive it. The pit is sunk from twenty to thirty feet deep, and then chambered at the bottom, that is, the pit-man digs or cuts out the chalk horizontally, in three separate directions: the horizontal apertures being of a sufficient height and width to admit of the pit-man's working in them with ease and safety. One pit will chalk six acres, laying sixty loads on an acre."

There was another Kentish practice which, though it has nothing to do with manuring, may be mentioned here, as it had a decided effect on the fertility of land; and that was flint-picking. The flints which thickly strewed the surfaces of the fields in many districts, must often have seemed useless encumbrances to the farmer, and when he was offered a good price for them by a builder or road-contractor (for surface-flints are tougher and much less brittle than quarried flints) he seldom refused it. There were always old women about, who were very glad to earn a few pence a day by picking flints; the flints were made into pyramidal heaps in the field and the work paid by the cubic yard. As they seemed to work up to the surface, a farmer at Stansted used to say that flints were his best crop. But it was a great mistake, for the flints held the moisture near the surface of the ground and greatly protected the roots of the crop, so that a field where they have been picked is damaged to a greater extent than is paid for by the price obtained for them.

Lime and soot are both used to a large extent by farmers, as they have been for centuries; the former in conjunction with animal manure and as a destroyer of insects and diseases of root-crops; the latter partly as a manure and partly to guard the crop against slugs and against worms, which will sometimes pull the young shoots under the ground as soon as they have sprung up. But there are fewer lime-kilns in every part of the country than there were ten years ago, for lime is of no use without manure.

When the barn-yard manure was carted out it was put in muck-heaps at the side of the field, and on it the lime was spread and the whole turned over, to destroy the seeds of weeds and other harmful things which might be in it; and this was a sounder plan than watering to promote fermentation, which is sometimes done now.

In heavy clay districts, in the Cambridgeshire fens, and throughout the western counties, there was another practice, called "Devonshiring" or burn-baking and by many other names. This consisted in paring off the surface, especially of an old pasture, and burning it in heaps over the field. The turf or stubble was generally cut off to a depth of from one to three inches with a breast-plough, though in Cambridgeshire, where there were not many stones, a horse-drawn paring-plough was used. Sometimes it was simply a way of getting rid of couch-grass, which in Gloucestershire was often left to grow at the headlands of a field till the ground was matted with it and then pared off, dried and burnt. In Wiltshire the couch parings were "stifle-burnt" and, together with the contents of the liquid-manure tank, used in the turnip drill. In other places it was done to lighten very heavy land, the charcoal and bricky fragments of burnt clay making the ground more porous, while the potash and other constituents of the organic parts were liberated for the use of the coming crop. Thus it was a means of turning fen-land into market-garden land, a way of preparing old worn-out pasture-land for tillage, and a rough and ready manner of manuring with ashes; but if overdone, or done on the wrong kind of soil, it could be very injurious to land, and it was in many farm leases forbidden to be practised oftener than once in seven years. The process was called paring and burning in the eastern counties, in the West burn-baking, burn-baiting, beat-burning, or Devonshiring, in Kent down-sharing or dentchering, though the last expression sometimes signified no more than the cutting off of old turf.

In Devonshire paring and burning took the form known as raftering or ribbing, which was, and sometimes is, practised here and elsewhere without the use of fire, for clearing old turf in preparation for tillage. It is done thus: the turf is pared across in alternate strips, a narrow width of it being alternately turned over and left untouched. The slice which is cut is laid over to cover the uncut strip, the turf surfaces facing one another and the upper one being somewhat wider and overlapping the lower so as to leave "room enough for a lark to roost"—such was the country saying. It was left thus for some months till the turf was partly decayed and then, if it were not raked into heaps and burnt, a spring-harrow or cultivator set to the depth of the first cut was drawn across it, and the lumps afterwards broken up and dispersed with drags and chain-harrows. This was sometimes called skirting.

If the soil were heavy, the turfs were twisted so as to stand on their edges and dry, and then burnt in the open all over the field, so that the soil was burnt too, but on light lands they were made into heaps of about the size of haycocks, with the turf downwards and with some straw or brushwood in the middle to light them, and after being fired were covered so as only to smoulder; by this means the earth would not be thoroughly calcined.

To return to the subject of manures; it is evident that the present conditions of labour have made it impossible for the farmer of the present day to fertilise his land by the methods which his grandfather was able to command. No longer, as in the days of high farming, is much heard of such powerful manures as furrier's clipping, fellmonger's poake, sugar-baker's scum, soap-boiler's ashes, sheep's trotters, horn-shavings, leather waste and scrawings, slaughter-house refuse, malt-dust, hog's hair and seal-hair. No doubt some of these materials are still obtainable, but at a price which would put them out of the reach of all but a few market-gardeners or nurserymen. Many farmers used to keep a pigeon-cote of considerable size and thus produced a great quantity of guano, such as is now bought at exorbitant prices; though whether it ever paid for the damage which the pigeons must have done on the farm is another matter. (Night-soil was up till the eighties or nineties available to farmers who cared to send for it to many of the larger towns, at a shilling the load; it was certainly one of the best manures, though not the most lasting in its effects.) There was a curious prejudice at some seaside places against putting locally caught fish on the fields, though indeed hundreds of tons of mackerel have been used on the farms between Winchelsea and Lewes, for the sheer impossibility of selling them all; but in some places it was thought that this would end the fishermen's luck. Sea-weed must be mentioned as another important manure; on the coast between Cork and Wexford, where much barley is grown, the long ribbony "fyowns" are considered especially good for this crop. Elsewhere they use cartloads of starfish, mussels and sprats, though the best authorities recommend making them into a compost with earth. In hop-gardens woollen rags are still used. Hop-litter is almost the only organic manure which has become more extensively used lately, and though it holds the moisture near the surface and generates some nitre, it is rather a poor one.

Artificial manures are incomparably easier and more pleasant to handle than most organic manures and they may contain the essentials of plant growth in higher proportion and in a readily assimilated form, but this the old-fashioned farmer would not admit. The prejudices against them arise from several causes. The first no doubt is his complete ignorance of the theory of chemistry, so that he may use manure which is unsuitable to his soil or crop or by mixing two or more produce a chemical reaction which will neutralise the effects of both. Another reason is that some firms sell mixed manures which are largely adulterated with worthless matter, and knowing this he may distrust an honest firm which would prescribe the right manure for his particular soil. He does not always understand the science of combining artificial manuring and green manuring, which has been so clearly explained by many modern authorities, though this will doubtless be gradually taught by county organisers, agricultural colleges and other expert advisers. It is still regarded, and with some reason, as a means of robbing the land, of unfairly stimulating and exploiting whatever goodness is there already and leaving it good for nothing. And so indeed it is, as it is practised by many farmers to-day. Not that the notion of getting more out of the land than is fairly put into it is at all a new one; but modern conditions make it much more tempting and some mechanical manures make it, for a time, much easier to do.

"Starve the land of labour and it will starve you."
This maxim puts the matter in a nutshell and is in fact
what all the old writers on husbandry continually em-
phasised. He who holds this view is not against new
inventions as such; if machinery were used for good
cultivation instead of for cutting down labour the results
would be better than before. He believes in machinery,
but not in doing away with labour. But now farmers
must pay more for labour than they can afford, hence
they employ less than they need.

Hedger's bill

Chapter V

SIGNS OF THE WEATHER

FORETELLING the weather was lately a rural art, practised more or less by every farmer and countryman; it has now become a civil science, the monopoly of learned specialists, whose oracles are broadcast to a respectful world. These modern prophets see changes and processes of world-wide scope; the older school of seers was in the main concerned with merely parochial phenomena.

The weathercock on every barn and steeple was naturally the first authority to be consulted, but to read its meaning aright was more than a rule-of-thumb matter; it was necessary to be guided also by local experience. Besides this source of knowledge, there were changes dependent on the stars and calendar, of which the well-known belief about Swithin's day is an example. The third and, if it be indeed a separate thing, by far the most important kind of understanding is that *sense* of the weather sometimes possessed by country people as a natural gift or faculty, as mysterious as the power of water-divining, blood-stanching, or of ready-reckoning by illiterate folk with no school knowledge of arithmetic: a sense more often acquired with rheumatism and corns. And though such understanding may not be teachable, a few country sayings may be recorded here, to serve as specimens of the traditionary interpretation of weathercock and calendar portents.

If the wind is in the wrong quarter when the sun "crosses the line" in March, it will be wet till June 24th.

"Sun setting with the wind against it" means rain.

A ring round the moon is the sign of a break in the

weather; the farther away the ring, the sooner the break will come.

"One night there was a star right in the pocket of the moon; I said then that we would have a storm, and the next day sure the whole place came crashing round us!"

S. Ireland.

When the wind changes from north or east to west or south here it is a sure sign of rain; if it changes the opposite way it is an equally certain promise of fine weather.

When the springs and wells are running over, it is a sign of clear fine weather; when they are dry or run low it is the sign of a break.

A dark line round the horizon in the evening means rain the next day.

A "wind-dog" or "weather-gall", that is, a small part of a rainbow in a cloudy sky means that there will be bad stormy weather.

When there are great white clouds, piled up like mountains, there will not be enough wind to turn a mill.

Kent.

Large separate clouds like flakes are a sign of heavy rain the next day.

If the moon is on its back or turning up it is a sign of rain. This is a saying which varies in form, some thinking that the moon on its back will hold the rain, and that when it begins to turn up it will spill the rain from it.

Norfolk.

"The new moon with the old moon in her arms" is often seen the night before a storm.

A red streaky sunset comes before a stormy, blustery day.

When it is going to rain, sometimes a day or two before the weather breaks, swallows and swifts fly close to the ground, black snails come out on the land in the daytime, and frogs go on to the roads and paths.

Beside the "ash and oak" saying, whose truth is so hard to prove or disprove—the oak budding first, but the leaves of ash expanding more quickly—there are other ways of foretelling a wet or dry season. If the moorhens build their nests high up the banks of ponds or in bushes, it will certainly be a wet summer; if close by the water, it will be dry. It is also said (though less infallibly) that a very heavy crop of hips and haws predicts a hard winter, while when there are few it will be mild; this being a provision of nature to keep the birds alive when the ground is frozen.

Chapter VI

PLOUGHING

"Herein we seem to instruct those that are best able to teach us; which might be true if they all spoke the same language: but there is such a Babel of confusion, as well in their terms and names of things, as there is in practice of the art of agriculture itself, that remove a husbandman but fifty or an hundred miles from the place where he hath constantly exercised his husbandry to another, and he shall not only admire their method and order in tilling the land, but also their strange and uncouth language and terms, by which they term their utensils, instruments or materials they use, so much differing from those used in the country where he dwells."

J. WORLIDGE (*Dictionarium Rusticum*. 1681).

THE styles of ploughing which are favoured in different parts of the country vary much, and with them the types of plough; these differences are a question of custom almost as much as of the needs of diverse soils and climates. The simplest way of attempting an intelligible description of the ploughman's work may be, first, to explain the ordinary beginning and then to consider different ways in which a field may be set out.

The field is measured up and marked out with branches, or feathers set in cleft sticks, according to the form in which the ploughing is to be done; a headland being allowed of about four yards from the hedge all round the field, on which the horses may turn, and the length and breadth of the remainder being stepped out, to decide where the ridges are to be made. The old-fashioned ploughman paced out his work with great exactness, knowing exactly when he had finished an acre. In the eastern counties an acre-staff or a nine-foot gad was sometimes used to check accurately the breadth of the stitches, or lands between the ridges; this method survived within the memory of old ploughmen, but is now abandoned. In Maidstone Agricultural Museum there is a ploughman's staff with crossed sights at the head, so that a rectangular piece of land can easily be determined.

In many parts of the country some form of "one-way" plough is now generally used; with this the ploughman may have nothing more to do than to drive successive furrows from one side of the field to the other, reversing his mouldboard at the end of each furrow, so that all are laid the same way, and finishing with but two headlands, at top and bottom of the field. But the common fixed plough, as it goes forward, can only turn the furrow-slice from left to right, the breast or mouldboard being on the right side of the plough and the ploughman walking on the unploughed land on the near, or left, side; the land-handle continuing in line with the beam and the furrow-handle being set out to the right. Hence the ploughman tells his horses to "come" or "go", as he means them to turn left or right.

The ploughman's cries, to turn or stop his horses, though strange and unintelligible to the townsman and often debased to hoarse inarticulate shouts, are instantly understood and obeyed by the team. Some of them are no doubt survivals of respectable antiquity; they are hardly the same in any two parts of the country and several versions of each may be heard in many of those districts from which they have not been finally banished by the unresponsive tractor. The following table, though far from complete, may serve to illustrate their variety:

District	To start	To stop	Turn right	Turn left
N. Norfolk	go on	whoa	wheesh	cop y holt cup yere

Sussex	—	—	gee wut
			oot (to hind
			  horse)
				tho wut
				ga' wut (to hind
				  horse)

I. of W.	—	—	wut	comeather
Berks	—	—	wug off	—
Dorset	—	—	get off	come here
N. Devon	come on	we	—	wug
Cornwall	gee up go on (name of horse)	woa *or* wey	gee off	way come here

This additional list is added from Morton's *Cyclopaedia of Agriculture* (1863).

Scotland	(name of horse)	wo stand	hupp gee haup hip weesh	hie comeather wynd vane vine
Yorks	gehup	wo-ho	gee gee-back gee-ho	half half-back woa-beck
Cheshire	—	whoi	height height	come-agin haw
Glos	—	wey	woot	coom-yeh
Kent	—	woa	woot gee-woot	woi
Hants	gee	wey	woag	come-hither

In starting to plough a field the usual plan is to take it in strips, called stitches or rigs, and making a "top" in the middle of each of these plough round them successively till all is done. On heavy clay these stitches will be narrow, consisting of eight, ten, twelve or fourteen furrows; on fairly light land the tops may be thirty yards or more apart.

Before making the tops, a line is first cut all round the field to mark the inside limit of the headlands. From a measured mark on this line to a stick set up at the opposite headland the ploughman opens a straight furrow (Fig. 1), returning in the same track so as to deepen it and lay a second furrow-slice on the other side (Fig. 2). This is called "opening a top". In a wet season, this may be done immediately after the harvest is carried, to give the land a chance to drain. The two furrow-slices have next to be thrown inwards against one another and so the horses are turned fromwards, or to the right, and return down the outer edge of the second furrow-slice (Fig. 3) and back along the edge of the first one (Fig. 4).

Thus the top is closed, and the ploughman continues working round it, taking out the ploughshare at the end of each furrow, turning "to'ards" at the headland, and putting in the share at the proper distance (say eight or ten inches) from his last cut on the other side. Having thus "gathered" thirty furrows on either side of the top, he proceeds to the next top, which may have been already made by another ploughman, if several teams are working in the same field, and thirty furrows being similarly gathered on either side of this, he will turn his horses the other way at the headland and "split off" the intervening space, crossing the unploughed land to the side of the next top and finishing at last with a hollow, or "open thorough", down the middle: the furrow-slices being laid away from it on either side.

If the field is all rectangular, nothing now remains but to plough the headlands, beginning at one corner of the ploughed part, and working outwards round and round till the plough is brought as close as possible to the edges of the field. But if the end of the field is oblique or irregular, so that a triangle is left within the headland, this is ploughed as a gore, scoot or goosset—the furrows being made parallel to those in the rest of the field and their lengths successively reduced till all is done. As these short furrows necessitate much stopping and turning of the team, the ploughman will often contrive to set out his field in such a way as will leave as few "short lands" as may be, and those if possible all in one place. The forms in which this may be done will be described later.

"To plough a straight furrow" has become a proverb —perhaps with the institution of ploughing matches— but the old furrows were often winding, in the form of a long double curve, and hence called S-lands. This is supposed to have been the Saxon form. These S-lands were general when the common-field system was in use, and their forms can still be traced in many fields long since laid down to grass. The winding furrows are said to have drained heavy land better than do straight ones, and they had these advantages, that a team of oxen or horses could walk in line down the bed of the open furrow without treading on the ploughed land and the plough could be drawn to the very end of the field while the team was turning. Very few S-lands indeed are worked now; there are, or were lately, a few in North Norfolk and the Lincolnshire and Yorkshire wolds, Braunton Great Field in North Devon, and Laxton in Nottinghamshire are still worked thus on the common-field system.

Some mention must be made here of those ancient terraced lands, mostly on the sides of chalk downs, called "cow-walks" in Essex and lynchets in Sussex, Wiltshire, Hampshire, Berkshire and elsewhere, of which much has been written by antiquarians, some of whom think that at each ploughing a furrow was taken off from the upper side and laid down at the lower side of each strip, by means of which they gradually got their form; though how exactly this was done, with the chalk but a few

inches below the original surface, needs some explaining.

In some parts of Essex, ploughing is done according
to the shape of the hedge, that is to say, with twisting
furrows. At Wimbish Green a field whose longest
boundary is in the form of an arc is still "ploughed
rainbow" as they say, so as to leave a few "short lands"
in one corner only, and a path which crosses this field
follows the same curve. Another similarly shaped field
in the next parish is called "Rainbow Shot".

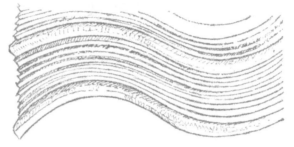

Fig. 5. "Rainbow"

To return to straight furrows, these, as has been said,
are made on heavy land in narrow stitches—stetches,
rigs or warps, as they are called in Essex, the north-
eastern counties, and Kent respectively. Making eight-
furrow stitches was known as "four-thoroughing"; the
hollow furrow between each one and the next served to
drain the land, and cross-furrows were made where
necessary to connect them and to lead the water to a
ditch at the side or bottom of the field. In Essex these
cross-drains are sometimes made first with a double-
breasted plough and then dug out deeper and smoother
with a slough or wooden spade. In the clay lands of
Norfolk the rigs had generally twelve furrows, while the
warps in Kent had fourteen furrows or seven "wents".

The tendency of late years has been to increase the number of furrows in each strip, partly to save labour in making tops and partly because, unless the land is very wet and heavy, so many furrows are really unnecessary. But the old method had the advantage of precision. The width of each furrow was regularly determined, and the rollers and sets of harrows were made of the right size to take the width of each strip. Seed-drills also were made of half the width of a warp, so that the wheel would run up one furrow and the horses also could walk up the furrow without treading on the ridges. The disadvantage of this method, however, is that it makes the ground uneven for the reaping-machine to work across, though the harrowing and rolling will have tended to flatten the ridges considerably.

Many other forms of ploughing are practised on light lands where draining is not so necessary and it is desirable to leave the surface as level as possible and without ridges or hollows.

If a field is wider at one end than at the other, it may be worked in what are sometimes known as French gores or scoots, that is, diminishing furrows inside the field instead of at the sides.

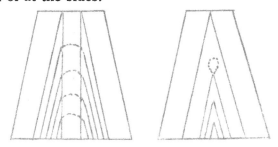

Fig. 6. "French"

In the first form of French gore a broad headland at each side of the field and another strip of equal width in the middle are marked off, leaving two triangular or tapering spaces which are to be ploughed first. The ploughman will start along the edge of the headland, turn his horses on the strip in the middle and plough back along the headland, then beginning a somewhat shorter furrow inside the first one, and so on till all the surface of these two strips is done. The headlands they plough one at a time, working towards the centre so as to throw the furrow outwards and to finish with a furrow down the middle of each. This done, the ordinary headland round the whole field may be ploughed, working from inside and finishing at the hedge.

In the second form of French gore two parts are cut off, parallel to the hedges and meeting at the smaller end of the field. The triangle thus marked off is then divided in half from the base, and a furrow opened down the middle. The ploughman then proceeds in short furrows on either side of this middle one, working from right to left and back again along the bottom of the field, and turning his horses at the central furrow as shown by the dotted line; thus all the furrows will be thrown inwards. This form is almost identical with what is called from its shape "heater-work", where a triangular field is

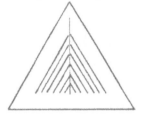

Fig. 7. "Heater-work"

ploughed first in the centre until a headland of equal width is left all round.

Another common form in Norfolk and Lincolnshire, especially useful for burying green manure, is "mill-sail" ploughing. The field is first cut across diagonally, and the middle of it worked in a short top. Then the ploughman works round and round this, turning at the diagonal cuts and throwing the furrow inwards until all the field is

finished. In a triangular or irregular field the cuts are
sometimes made to bisect the corners and meet in the

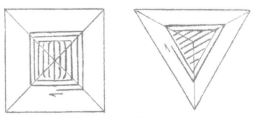

Fig. 8. "Mill-sail"

middle, but as it is almost necessary to make a top or
scoot in the middle, this differs but little from heater-
work.

Round-ploughing is a very similar method, though
considered old-fashioned by some ploughmen. In one

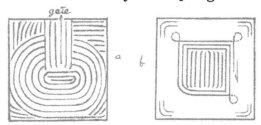

Fig. 9. "Round-ploughing"

form of round-ploughing a strip is left from the gate
to the middle of the field, and from the end of this
strip the furrows are "gathered" round and round, the
strip from the gate being left unploughed till the very
end, as a headland for the horses to turn upon. As the
corners are reached scoots are made, finishing one at a
time, just enough room having been left for another
furrow to get to the next corner. Last of all the strip of
land from the gate is ploughed, being "split off" or
worked from the inside outwards till a single furrow is

left from the middle of the field to the gate. Often three or four teams will follow one another round the field.

In another form, which is really only a variety of mill-sail ploughing, a short top is made in the middle, enough furrows gathered against it to form a square (or a rectangle of the same proportions as the field) and ploughing is continued round it. At three corners the horses are turned *outwards*, on the unploughed land, while the fourth is left as a "rounding-corner". When the team gets so close to the hedges that there is no longer room to turn outwards, all four corners are made "rounding-corners", in the ordinary manner of ploughing head-lands.

Sometimes round-ploughing is done inwards from the outside of the field, and it is called "ploughing to the hedge", because the furrow-slice is turned outwards. In this way the ploughman finishes with a straight furrow in the middle, running in the direction of the longer sides of the field.

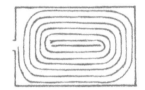

Fig. 10. "Ploughing to the hedge"

In practice no form of ploughing is quite as simple as those just enumerated, for most fields have more or less irregular or wavy outlines, which must be followed in working the headlands; or where this is not practicable the ploughman must allow small scoots where necessary, his chief concern being to plough straight wherever possible and not to go over any part twice, nor to turn his horses on the ploughed parts where it can possibly be avoided.

Where large wheel-ploughs were used which could not get quite close to the edges of a field, a swing-plough was and is sometimes still kept to do the last three or four furrows. But even then a farmer of the old school would not be content till the corners of the field, which the plough could not take, had been dug by hand.

It has seemed worth while to describe, in perhaps tedious detail, the simplest use of a plough and several old ways of setting about the work of ploughing. But to deal thoroughly with the many other ways in which furrows may be made is outside the scope of this book; they depend upon local requirements of soils and crops and are well understood and practised by modern agriculturists. Henry Stephens, in his *Book of the Farm* (1855), mentions as among the different methods of ploughing: "gathering up, crown and furrow, casting or yoking or coupling ridges; cleaving down ridges, cleaving down ridges with gore-furrows; ploughing two-out-and-two-in; ploughing in breaks; cross-furrowing" ("over-warting" in Norfolk); "angle-ploughing, ribbing and drilling". In Kent there is a process called "broom-striking", which consists of marking lines with the Kent plough, using the ordinary chisel-shaped point or share without the wreest. Where it is desired to plough land deeply, subsoiling is done: one plough turning a furrow-slice in the ordinary way, and another following immediately with a share but no mouldboard, thus breaking up and loosening the lower earth in the floor of the furrow, before it is covered by the next furrow-slice. To stir and loosen the surface of the ground a very broad round-edged share is used in Kent and Sussex; and the process is called spuddling. Some farmers in Berkshire and elsewhere use a broad cutting-share for thistles; but there are endless shapes of share and turn-furrow, adapted to every conceivable use—each local foundry making dozens and the larger firms making hundreds of different patterns.

The actual shape of the section of each furrow is determined primarily by the construction of the ploughshare and mouldboard, its depth and width by the setting of the plough. A most important thing for a ploughman to understand is how to set his plough; in this term are included the adjustment of the coulter-blade and share—the breadth of two fingers is usually allowed as the proper distance between the two points—the raising or lowering of the share so as to plough to exactly the right depth, the rake or inclination of the plough to one side if necessary, the proper distribution of the draught between the horses according to their strength, and the adjustment of the mouldboard, if that is a moveable one. Different fields, and even different parts of a single field, may need a different setting of the plough, the draught varying with the heaviness of the soil and the depth of ploughing. (The draught is said to be proportioned to the square of the depth of land ploughed; so that, for example, the ratio of the draught at three inches to that at six would be as nine to thirty-six: if the former needed the whole strength of one horse, four horses would be required for the latter.)

Ploughing matches, which are still quite popular events, have played an important part in the evolution of modern ploughs, though Henry Stephens, writing in 1860, was of the opinion that the judges of ploughing matches were inclined to encourage superficial neatness rather than thoroughness of work. These matches take place generally in October, but with the recent decline in arable farming they are not the great affairs they once were; and with their present heavy expenses farmers cannot afford to give their men the time off, while the men themselves find other amusements. Formerly they had a whole day for it, and each man ploughed a half-acre strip; now they plough only a furrow or two, and all is over in half a day.

I cannot resist the temptation to copy out, from the Bath Society's papers of 1795, this report of an old ploughing match, which seems to give a notion of the spirit in which it was undertaken.

"We the umpires chosen for determining the Premiums given by the Bath Society for Ploughing this day do adjudge the said premiums as follows.

1st Premium to Mr DYKE's two-furrow plough with four horses, as the best and cheapest plough for general use, and do recommend the same as a saving both of men and horses: though, from a fault in the construction of the plough produced to-day, the furrows were not laid sufficiently flat.

2nd Premium. To Mr THOMAS's single-wheel plough with two horses: and we do recommend the said plough, as having performed exceedingly well on a stiff heavy soil.

3rd Premium. To Mr PRITCHARD's plough with two horses without a driver, as being a plough better adapted for stiff heavy soil than the general ploughs of the country. And the ploughman of the other competitor, Mr GID-DINGS, having done his best with an aukward bad-constructed plough of the county, we think proper to order him a gratuity of five shillings.

> H. J. Close.
> Stephen Neate.
> William Short.
> Thomas Davis.
> Thomas Lewis.

LOCAL PLOUGHS AND PLOUGH-MAKERS

Having given some account of the ploughman's work, I will briefly describe a few of the older types of plough, made by country blacksmiths and carpenters, which still hold their own in some districts against the products of modern science. Whatever may be urged against the obstinacy of those farmers who refuse to adopt new methods, the fact remains that some of the traditional types of plough do their work better, if more slowly, and are more perfectly adapted to local conditions than the "cheap, speedy and efficient" contrivances which are advertised to supplant them.

No doubt, owing to the extremely bad state of the roads in many parts of the country till well within the last half-century, some very rude methods long continued to exist here and there. The cas-chrom, a primitive tool between a spade and a plough, worked by one man, was until fairly lately the implement of tillage in the Isle of Skye; while the phrase "to chip a plough"— meaning to cut a plough-beam out of a suitably-grown tree—is understood to this day by old labourers and "rough carpenters" in Dartmoor, some of whom have probably themselves done it in years gone by.

But those local forms of plough which yet remain in use represent more mature traditions of craftsmanship. The Norfolk wheel-plough has changed but little since the eighteenth century; and it is still possible to travel for miles in North Norfolk, when ploughing is being done, and hardly meet with a single example of any other sort.

Some reference has already been made to the turn-wrest plough traditionally used in Kent and Sussex: the oldest, and one of the best, of the several forms of one-way plough. It consists of a straight beam some ten feet long, mortised at the hinder end into the *stump*, to which at either side the short, curved handles are fixed. The lower end of the stump is joined to the horizontal *chep*, a piece of wood about four feet long which forms the

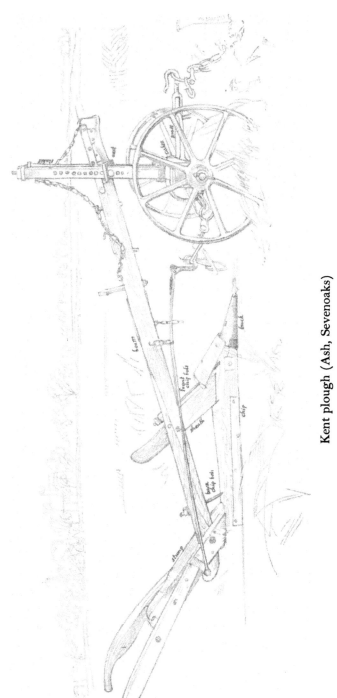

Kent plough (Ash, Sevenoaks)

base of the plough, and to whose forward end is fixed the iron *buck* or socket which carries the share. Immediately behind the coulter is a flat piece of wood called the *sheath*; this is mortised through both chep and beam. The head of the beam can be raised or lowered on a wooden *pillow* which is adjusted by pins between two stakes, which rise vertically from the *eakes* or axle in front. The wheels are about three feet high and nowadays are sometimes made of cast-iron, but the old sort have heavy wooden naves and spokes whose ends are fixed by *collars* and *sprigs* to the narrow iron *tren* which forms the circumference of each wheel. The horses are attached to the iron *pratt*, which projects forward from the eakes, the latter being directly fastened to the hinder part of the plough by the *draught-chain*.

The mouldboard, or, as it is variously called, the *wrest*, *wreest*, *riste* or *rice*, is a long, somewhat rounded plank, not twisted like other mouldboards, and at the end of each furrow it can be pulled off the *spindle* which holds it to the chep and fixed upon the other side of the plough. At the same time the point of the coulter, which is fixed somewhat loosely in its mortise, is shifted across by reversing the position of a cudgel called the *road-batt* (used also for cleaning the plough) which lies on the top of the beam, secured between the *cock-pin*, the round end of the coulter, and the head of the sheath.

A strong thill-horse is needed to pull the share out at the end of each furrow, and a team of six may be required to draw it on heavy land. But though it may seem ungainly and has excited the envious ridicule of many agricultural writers since Cromwell's time, the turn-wrest plough does its work extremely well and by many farmers who have used it is praised for its great adaptability. It does equally well with several different forms of share: with boards nailed on to either side, called *hogs* or *shelve-ristes*, it will serve for ridging turnips or earthing up potatoes; with the addition of a seed-box it can be used for drilling beans or "sowing under the furrows"; while by some farmers the eakes were even taken off and used on a wider sort of bean-drill.

In many places the turn-wrest has given way to the balance-plough, an invention of the middle of last century; its parts are duplicated in reverse, one half being always in the air and pressing down its counterpart. The double beam forms an angle, at which is a two-wheeled axle, drawn by a chain. When the horses are turned at the end of the furrow this chain is run over and the plough is pulled in the opposite direction; the upright part is brought down to the ground and the one which has just been ploughing serves in turn as an equipoise. The two mouldboards face one another like an object and its reflection in a mirror, so that as the horses follow down the first furrow, the second is turned over in the same direction. Multi-furrowed ploughs, drawn by steam-power, are generally made on this principle.

Of other one-way ploughs than these, there are used in Cornwall and Devon several versions of turnover plough, similar in principle to the Brabant plough whose two mouldboards revolve on a horizontal beam, and the American Oliver's plough. To these must be added a two-pointed plough, known formerly in South Devon as a "one-way zuel", and developed by Lowcock, Chamberlain and other makers.

Wooden swing-ploughs are still made in Essex and used by most of the smaller farms in the heavy clay districts of that county. The land-handle of these ploughs continues in a straight line with the beam and is occasionally even part of the same piece of timber; and the furrow-handle is often a straight rough stake which passes beneath the mouldboard and is inserted into sockets in the slade or ground-wrest. Thus it clearly illustrates the development of the primitive one-handled plough.

Swing-ploughs are used in but few other parts of South and West England; though here and there the work of a local maker has been so well adapted to the particular needs of the neighbouring farmers that his ploughs have survived till recent years and are sometimes used even at the present day. Such ploughs are, or have been within the last few years, used in Essex, Yorkshire, Hertfordshire, Cambridgeshire, Surrey, parts of Kent and Sussex, Wiltshire and Warwickshire, and doubtless in several other localities. A common wooden swing-plough of traditional design has for the last sixty years and until recently been made by Mr Benj. Heatheridge, at the village of Maisemore near Gloucester. It has a cast-iron share and "sheldboard", as the turn-furrow is called. The latter is deep, rounded, and adapted for digging, and was made by a foundry in Gloucester. They were first used in place of wooden ones by the father of the present maker. Six horses have sometimes been used to force this plough through heavy clay, and the plough has stood this very unfair strain. The price is £7. Mr Heatheridge has one left on hand, but intends to make no more.

A still more curious survival is a wooden foot-plough, made by Mr Hiscock, wheelwright and carpenter of Horton near Devizes, which is illustrated. Its share, which is of wrought-iron, is typical of those which were generally used in the eighteenth century, being composed of a long bar which was bolted on to the ground-wrest, and a fin some inches from the point, which is

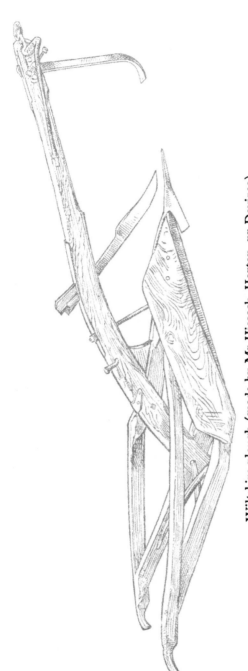

Wiltshire plough (made by Mr Hiscock, Horton, nr Devizes)

chisel-shaped. This, with the other plough-irons, namely the drail or hake, coulter, ratch-pin and foot, are made by the local smith. The foot is a bent piece of iron mortised through the beam near its front end, capable of being adjusted higher or lower, and secured with a wedge; on this the plough bears instead of on wheels, and its regulation has a similar effect in determining the depth of ploughing. Its shape is drawn out, not by eye as with the Maisemore plough, but by means of patterns or templets of thin board, which have existed probably ever since the plough was first designed, which may have been during the late eighteenth century. The mouldboard —called here the broad-board—is specially interesting, since it is not straight or slightly curved like most wooden mouldboards, but is sawn out of a log so as to have a twist. A log five feet long and nine inches deep is fixed over the saw-pit and plumbed down the middle of each end. Marks are made at two inches distance from the top and bottom of either line in alternate directions, and these are joined with four straight lines, which are thus the boundaries of a symmetrically twisted plane. It is sawn out by a two-handled saw; the top sawyer keeping his eye on the upper line, and the bottom sawyer following the lower one. Thus one surface of the broad-board is made, and a similar cut marked at two inches distance from the first completes the twisted slice of wood; and as many more may be cut as the width of the log will allow. But before the broad-board can be fixed to the plough its upper and under edges must be adzed to a central line, and its ends shaped to fit the share and ground-wrest. The mouldboards used to be sawn out for 1s. 6d. each; now it would cost 4s. The present cost of the plough is £5—formerly it was less—so it compares favourably with that of an iron plough, which in this district is thought to be less efficient. It must be owned, however, that this symmetrically twisted mould-board is not the most efficient or the lightest in draught. The best forms of mouldboard follow the shape of the turning furrow-slice and are thus more sharply curved forward than behind.

The development of the science of plough-making in the late eighteenth and early nineteenth centuries by Foljambe, Small, Arbuthnot and Ransome, has been ably chronicled by Mr J. B. Passmore; but it may be mentioned here that, as in other such evolutions, empirical knowledge generally preceded mathematical calculation. The iron ploughs of Ransome and Howard followed none of the wooden types in their lines, but by means of an endless variety of shares and turn-furrows, designed to suit particular needs, they contrived to do work of the kind required in many different districts. Messrs Ransome employed a team of horses and two very skilful ploughmen to take part in plough matches all over the country; and in this way learned the local needs by practical experience. A few firms, however, adapted the local type of plough to iron construction; this was done in some places with the Norfolk and Kent ploughs, and other examples are the jack-plough which is used on the Berkshire Downs, and another plough sometimes used in Hampshire which combines the principles of the gallows-plough and the jack-plough. Many of these ploughs were made by country foundries, which also supplied blacksmiths with cast-iron shares and turn-furrows. These foundries often had a water-wheel to work the furnace-bellows and could undertake work which was quite outside the scope of the ordinary smith, who is concerned only with wrought-iron. Often they were of some antiquity; and although there are one or two left in Berkshire, they have mostly disappeared since the making of implements has been more and more restricted to a few large firms. In North Wales, however, ploughs are usually made by local smiths, and generally follow a graceful double curve from handles to hake, instead of having the straight beam and handles which are characteristic of most English iron ploughs. The turn-furrows and shares are supplied by the foundry; the latter in the form of wrought-iron "blanks", which are beaten into shape by the blacksmith. These shares will not break as cast-iron shares will, but as the ground is very stony they are soon worn and blunted; and so at the end of every week the ploughman may have to take one or two to the smithy to be re-plated, and fix fresh ones to the ploughs on Monday.

When wooden ploughshares were given up in the West of England, the making of iron ploughs often came into the hands of the blacksmiths who had formerly made the plough-irons only. Some few of the smiths who specialised in this work made local reputations and founded firms which lasted for some time, though gradually only the larger and more progressive of them survived.

Failure in such undertakings is often more picturesque than success of the kind loved by advertisers and celebrated by Samuel Smiles; for the cunning workman is seldom one whose tastes and temperament qualify him for success in building up a business. An instance of this kind may be allowed. At Earthcott in Gloucestershire there was a smithy where ploughs were made; it has been given up for many years, though John Savery, once the master of it, is still living and a very skilful smith. His father and grandfather had been well-known plough-makers, and he himself was born under the roof of a

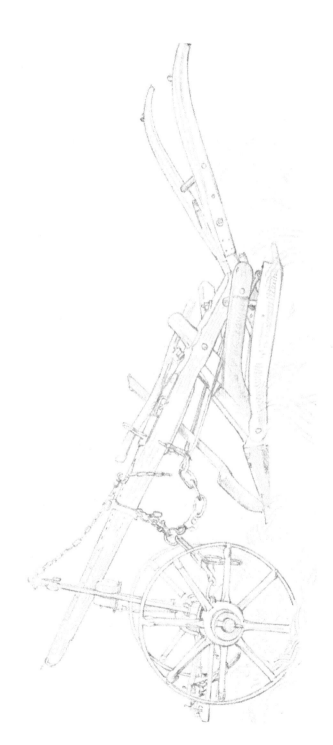

Sussex plough (Pyecombe)

smithy and so, as he said, he never found plough-making a difficulty—it came natural to him. There is a beautiful little model plough, not two feet long, which he made before he was twenty, by hammering up old horse-nails —nobody can guess how and it would be hard for him to explain. Ploughs which he made twenty years ago are to be seen on some farms, still capable of good service.

Savery's plough was designed to go on one wheel, but this could be removed and a pair bolted instead to the beam. Though inclined to be heavy, it was very steady and well-balanced, requiring but little guidance. It was made so truly that it could be set in position and drawn down the furrow without being touched, so that a ploughman who should drop his whip might run back and pick it up without stopping the horses. A special point of the design was the "drail" or hake, to which the draught-chain was fastened by a pin in a double set of holes at right angles to the beam, instead of the usual shallow-indented rack. By this means, it was claimed, the plough could be raked over and used for "bouting-up" (or leaving nearly upright furrows) as no other such plough could be.

When these ploughs were first made they had, I believe, wrought-iron shares and hammered mould-boards; but later, when cast-iron shares began to be used everywhere, the ploughwright bought wholesale Y.L. and Y.D. shares, which have the great advantage of being harder beneath than above, so that they always wear to a sharp edge. In this way his ploughs could be used on farms at a great distance, without the necessity of sending back to Earthcott whenever new shares were wanted. Savery designed two turn-furrows to fit these, a short bluff one for digging or spring ploughing and another for shallower autumn work; and he himself made the wooden patterns for the presses in which they were to be shaped and cast them in sand. These castings, which were very heavy, were bolted to great baulks of wood; and the turn-furrows (bought by the gross as flat "blanks" from the Sheffield rolling-mills) were heated

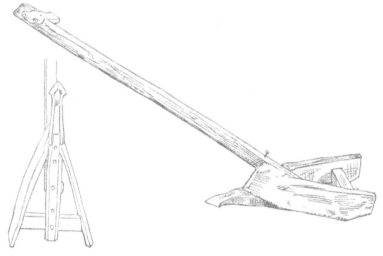

Hand-plough (West Hythe)

in a double fire and then screwed down between the blocks; a process not unlike those used by the largest firms.

There was a certain local champion ploughman, who said to John Savery, "Make I a plough, and do 'e take extra trouble over en, for I've got planty of money to pay for en, and I'll take and plough the whole world with your plough!" And so he did, winning prizes against all other ploughmen using the best-known makes until, as the smith put it, "One day a certain big firm—

what d'e think they done? Shall I tell 'e? Why, they took and give en a large purse o' money to do away wi' my plough—not to use en against theirn!''

BREAST-PLOUGHS

These tools were used extensively thirty or forty years ago, for paring turf and for burying stubble, but they are now almost extinct. In Somerset and Gloucestershire it was, till the end of the nineteenth century, not uncommon for eight or ten men to be employed on a field together, pushing the blades under the surface to a depth of two or three inches and turning over a thin broad slice. The breast-plough most commonly used had a stout handle from six to eight feet long, often with a downward curve near the blade end, and a fork at the handle end, the ends of which were mortised into a cross-piece, broad in the middle and with a rounded handle at either side. The blade was broadly pointed, about a foot long and up to eighteen inches wide; the left side had a ''counter'' or flange, turned up at right angles, by which the edge of the slice was cut; and both sides were straight and parallel for a few inches, when they curved inwards to a point in front. The beam or handle was fixed in the socket of the blade by a cleat or wooden wedge.

The man who used this implement wore ''beaters'', made of patches of horse-hide with strips of wood fastened lengthwise to them, to protect his thighs. By pushing these against the cross-handle and exerting his weight, he forced the blade along for a couple of feet, then turning the handles over and taking a step forward for the next dig. Sometimes there was a short length of withy-wood fixed to the breast-plough to help in turning over the turf, one end of it being split and fixed over the counter, the other nailed to the beam. For the same purpose, where the soil was loose, two small boards were sometimes fixed behind the blade, on either side of the beam.

Breast-plough (Mr Abraham Holder, North Wraxall, Wilts, 3 February 1931)

Some of the breast-ploughs used in Wiltshire were pushed from the groin, and to a forward curve in the beam a rope was attached, which another man pulled, thus cutting the slice continuously and greatly lightening the work. Various other names were given in other places to these implements; in Scotland they were called "slaughter-spades", in Kent "dentcher-ploughs", and in parts of Hereford, where they were used by O'Connor's Chartists, they were known as "betting-irons". There were several different types; two are used by the Exmoor turf-cutters, and those which were used in Lincolnshire, and for cutting off "emmet-casts" in Kent, were different again. A very rudimentary one was in use in 1930 at Bere Regis; it was simply a sort of shovel with a wide curved cutting blade turned slightly upwards. The beam was a thick stick with a natural curve near the socket and a short handle like that of an ordinary shovel, and the tool was used in much the same way, the worker pressing with the inside of his right knee against the back of his hand, to get a better purchase against it. It was used for cutting the turf with which, together with wood, the blacksmith made a ring of fire for heating the tires of cart-wheels.

Chapter VII

SOWING

IT is almost inevitable to think of a sower as one who scatters the seed broadcast on the furrows, like the sower in the parable. This must be an art as old as husbandry, but it is not now so familiar a sight as formerly. The sower marks the breadth of his cast with a stick at the headland, at the correct distance on his left side, and walks towards another one set up at the opposite side of the field; on reaching this he moves it to mark a new strip of the same width and returns to the first one. If the field is on a hill he will set up an intermediate stick on the rising ground in the middle. The seed is generally carried in a large kidney-shaped basket or box slung at the left side of the sower, while he throws it with his right hand as he paces across the field; as he returns, he pushes the seed-lip round to his right side and sows with his left hand. This seed-lip, otherwise called a seed-cot, hopper or scuttle, was made of thin wooden boards, bent to the required shape, like the old gallon and peck measures, but it is not common to meet with a wooden one now; galvanised iron vessels have taken their place. A sowing-sheet or looped-up bag was sometimes used instead.

In most of the eastern counties broadcast sowing has been abandoned, and wheat is now put in with a drill, but it is in quite common use in the West and North. Scotch farmers make their men sow with both hands alternately, so as to cover twice the ground in the time. The cast is made inwards; if with the right hand, the seed is thrown from right to left, descending in a curve with surprising evenness. Each cast is made in time with the step, with a steady and deliberate swing, and the experienced sower can regulate the amount with great nicety, so as to distribute exactly a given quantity, whether large or small, to every acre.

There is a tool for broadcast sowing called a fiddle, which has been known in the West of England for seventy or eighty years and is to be seen on some farms in Gloucestershire, Somerset and Dorset. It has a hopper from which the seed flows into some cups or paddles which can be whirled round; they turn on a spindle, round which a bowstring is looped, and as the bow is drawn backwards and forwards (like a fiddle-bow) the seed is flung out with a centrifugal impulse. There seems to be little to recommend this tool beyond the fact that it sows on both sides and needs less skill to use; it can scarcely be easier to judge the quantity sown by it than by hand.

It was a universal custom to sow according to the calendar, not only in this country, but in all ancient civilisations. Winter wheat was sown in the "darks of November" or, in some places, of October, to grow with the moon. It was usual to sow either when there was no moon or at a new moon, or at least when the moon was on the wax; and Arthur Young mentions as exceptional a successful farmer who sowed spring wheat "in the wane of April". The East Anglian farmers seem to be the only ones who now take notice of the moon in sowing; most farmers are inclined to ridicule the notion, yet there are signs that modern science may revive it. The faith of some old Welsh farmers knew no bounds: rams were put to ewes, settings of eggs put under the hen, and pigs killed, on the increase of the moon; if the last were duly done, the meat would swell, but if the beast were slaughtered in the wane, it would dwindle.

There is a saying that it is "no good looking for mush-rooms after full moon, they don't grow except with the moon". On the other hand an old countryman in Kent used to declare, of ferreting for rabbits, that "they will bolt from their holes when the moon is wasting, for then they have the sign in their heels; but when she is making they have the sign in their heads, and then they will sit fast".

"When you hear the first chapter of Genesis in church, put in your oats": that is, at Septuagesima. In Essex, if all the drilling were finished by Good Friday, the farmer's wife gave the men a seed-cake tea; and in Lincolnshire the end of sowing (about the second week of October) was celebrated with a "frummity supper". By many people, potatoes are planted on Good Friday afternoon; in South Devon it was said, "We sow our potatoes at the foot of the Cross".

When the seed is sown on the furrow, as it is with broadcast sowing, it must with all speed be harrowed in and otherwise protected from the rooks and other birds, which are nearly as mischievous coming after the sower as they are useful when they follow the plough. Bird-scaring—in Kent it is called "bird-minding" by the old people—was the labourer's earliest task; boys of seven or eight used to do it for a shilling a week, though in some places they got as much as fourpence or fivepence a day. They were seldom provided with rattles; they might have some pebbles to shake in a tin, but often they had simply to shout. The board-schools have done away with much of this wholesome employment; even in the holidays such labour commands a higher price. The occasional report of a decrepit firelock may now startle the echoes, but science has otherwise made little change in this department of agriculture. The withered corpses

of rooks are hung on sticks about the fields; and near
towns, where old clothes are plentiful, there is generally
a goodly population of scarecrows: "dudmen", as they
were once called. Pigeons attack the peas especially and
will almost clear a field of them if given a chance. An
old trick of Kentish farmers was to string one or two
peas on long threads, with bits of paper tied to the ends
like the tail of a kite. The unlucky bird which swallowed
a tethered pea would fly off with the train of paper
following it, furiously pursued by the rest of the flock,
which for a long time would be wary of entering that
field again.

There are worse enemies than birds in the field, and
these not so easily dealt with, since they work in secret;
that is to say wireworms, slugs and grubs. To protect
the seed against these and against blight, the old method
was to steep it in strong brine or chamber-lye, to skim
off and reject the grains which floated, and to dry the
rest by mixing them with lime or wood-ashes; but this
excellent plan is seldom followed now. Rolling does
much to destroy wireworms; soot keeps off slugs and
earthworms.

For sowing grass and clover seed there is a seed-
barrow, with a large narrow-rimmed wheel, and carrying a box or trough fifteen feet long. This is divided into
sections which are filled with seed, and as the barrow is
pushed, a gear from the axle turns a spindle which runs
from end to end of the box; and on this are mounted
brushes which, as they revolve, sprinkle the seed regularly out of small holes in the bottom of the trough.
This is an old invention and is used on many farms; it is
sometimes pushed by one man, sometimes with another
man in front to share the weight. But there is an older
invention still, which consists of the box only; a man had

to carry it up and down the field shaking it as he went. There is one of these at a farm near Taunton, but it exists as a curiosity only.

Broadcast sowing is the only kind for which the ground is prepared by ploughed furrows, so that the seed falls into the hollows and is covered by raking the crests over it. For the other methods of sowing which have next to be considered—dibbling and drilling—the ploughed land is first harrowed and then lightly rolled.

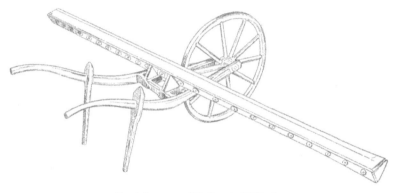

Seed-barrow (Tollard, Wilts)

DIBBLING

Dibbling is the method of sowing by making holes in the ground at regular intervals and dropping one seed or more into each hole. It is practised in setting out young plants of turnip, beet, etc., and sometimes for potatoes, beans and peas.

The dibbling of wheat and barley was introduced in the seventeenth and developed in the eighteenth century, when it was specially in use in Norfolk and Suffolk and in the other eastern counties. In the first half of the nineteenth century it was partly superseded by the drill method, but it was still considered to be the method which gave the best results and it was practised on some farms, and especially by seed-growers, till the end of the nineteenth century. It is still possible that it might be seen on some remote small-holding, though few labourers grow any wheat in this country, as so little bread is made at home.

The tool which was used for dibbling corn was an iron rod about three feet long with a handle like that of a spade and a pointed knob at the other end. A labourer with a dibble in each hand would walk backwards across the field making two rows of holes at a distance of six or eight inches between the rows and the same distance or less between each successive hole. As each pair of holes was made he would give a twist to the handles of the dibbles, to leave a clean hole. The Norfolk labourers used to cross their hands at the wrists, so as to keep an even distance between the rows; in Suffolk, instead of this, the feet were brought together at each step backwards, and the points of the dibbles were set against the toes; in Lancashire and Yorkshire the pair were sometimes linked together. In Norfolk the work was called "dabbling", in Suffolk and Essex it was usually "dibbing". The man's wife and child, or sometimes two children, followed him as he made the holes and dropped into each hole three kernels of wheat. Such work as this their smaller and more sensitive hands were much better able to perform than those of men, and they dropped the right number of seeds into each hole with great precision and speed. Many labourers who are still at work have spent weeks on this job and sometimes relate that after dibbling all day the children were so tired and sleepy that they had to carry them home.

A semi-mechanical dibbler was invented, probably in the first half of the nineteenth century, which was carried by one man and worked by setting it down on the ground and treading on a bar. It sowed in six holes at a time, but can hardly have saved any time or labour, for it was extremely heavy and cumbersome; and it was never widely adopted.

Broad beans are dibbled in ones or twos, peas in twos, threes or fours to each hole. In this work the dibble is short and with a heavier knob. It is used in the right hand, while the sower carries his seed in a bag at his waist and drops it into the holes with his left. To a practised man it seems as though the right number of peas comes each time to his fingers, and yet, though right-handed, he cannot drop them in easily or in regular numbers with his right hand, or even with his left unless he is at the same time using the dibble with his right. This illustrates curiously the subconscious, almost instinctive mechanical skill which a constantly repeated process of this kind develops.

The old way of marking the rows was to walk up the ridges dragging one foot so as to leave a little straight furrow. But it is now usual to make them with a machine, a marker of such a width that the wheels and the two horses go up the furrows on either side of the ridge. A row of vertical spikes projects from its frame to the ground, and these can be fitted with blades to make it into a horse-hoe; but for this work small angle-blades are attached, the vertical edge of each directed forward, and thus all the rows in a ridge are marked at once. As soon as possible after the seed is put in it must be covered; a wooden hand-rake is used on small seed-plots, but a set of three harrows is the thing for a field.

The root dibble is yet a different tool, being no more than a bent stick or handle with an iron point. In dibbling root-plants it is usual for a boy or a woman to drop them at equal distances along the rows, while several men follow picking up the plants and setting them in the rows.

Perhaps it should be added that a spiked disc or roller was invented for making the holes in which to plant potatoes, but it seems not to have met with much success.

DRILLING

Seed-drills were first brought into prominence about the middle of the eighteenth century by the celebrated Jethro Tull of Shalbourne, Berkshire, who also introduced horse-hoes; but it was not until the end of the century that his example was at all widely followed. The later history of their development it is not necessary to detail here; the main modern types have been in use for fifty or sixty years. Drills are provided with a row of coulters or shares, with a hole or shoot behind each, through which seed, or seed and manure, are projected into the grooves left by them. Small drills, which are pushed by hand, are used for beans in Kent, and in Norfolk little hand-drills called "dodgers", to fill in the gaps. The old Suffolk drill is the most imposing in appearance; it is designed to sow turnip-seed mixed with ashes and liquid manure. It is drawn by three horses and requires two men and a boy to work it, one to lead the horses, one to work the bar-handle in front of the drill, and one to walk behind and see that it is sowing evenly. Manure distributors are made on the same lines as seed-drills.

On cold and wet soils, seed is sometimes ploughed in, by having a hopper on the beam of the plough and a hollow shoot behind the share, for the seed to fall down; this is an old method, called "sowing under the furrow".

HARROWS

There are many sorts of harrow; the implements which generally go by that name are light and small, they are worked in pairs, or in sets of three or four, and are used for covering the seed when it is sown. In their simplest and most ancient form they are rectangular frames of crossed parallel timbers, with vertical tines at their intersections. In this shape, with wrought-iron tines and a diagonal strip of iron ending in a hook or "bull" by which to draw them, they are made by many village carpenters and blacksmiths in Kent. For covering grass-seed lighter harrows with numerous short wooden teeth are occasionally to be seen in the same county, but they are no longer made. Another primitive harrow, which consists of a wooden baulk pressing upon several thorn-bushes, is still used on grass, though largely superseded by chain-harrows. In one particular job, however, the bush-harrow is not beaten; it is excellent for breaking up the crust of mud which after rain sometimes tends to choke the young shoots of turnips.

Harrows are drawn by the corners, or at any rate obliquely, in order that the paths of their tines may be as close together as possible. For this reason where harrows were used in sets, that is, three or four fastened on a pole or "rider" to take the width of a ridge, they were made, at the beginning of the eighteenth century, in a slightly oblique form, or wider behind than in front. Later in the century zigzag iron harrows were invented, such as are now common. The usual plan, where the land was ploughed in ridges, was to harness the horses on either side, so that they should walk up the furrows without treading on the ridges, but there are many local differences of practice. In Scotland the harrows were sometimes fastened to a long beam supported on two cart-wheels and drawn by two horses walking tandem at either end. In most other places swing-trees, or as they are locally called lantreys, bodkins, hostreys or whipple-trees are used. In Berkshire there are two horses in line and one at the side, the old name for this being a "unicorn team"; in Suffolk three horses abreast; in Kent, on the lighter land, two, with a "twin-pole" between their bridles to keep them at the proper distance apart.

The work of the larger sorts of harrows, which generally go by the name of drags, is to prepare the soil for the seed, by breaking up the clods and raking out the roots of couch-grass and other weeds. In Kent they also are made with square wooden frames; in Norfolk they are wooden and triangular, with handles by which they can be guided or raised and with their tines directed forwards, and these are the prototypes of the three-wheeled iron scufflers.

CULTIVATORS

Grubbers, and various types of cultivators with moveable teeth, began to be introduced in the late eighteenth and early nineteenth centuries; more recently disc-harrows have come into general use. Cultivators, scufflers and scarifiers are closely related; the work of the first often takes the place of the later ploughings, while the last named is used to weed between the growing rows of wheat. Horse-hoes are used to weed and to loosen the surface soil, between rows of turnips or other plants; skim-ploughs are made on the same principle and have been in use for over a century in the West. They consist of a frame with two large adjustable horizontal blades, directed forwards and inwards, which loosen the surface in the same way as broad-sharing. These are a development of the eighteenth-century skim, which had a single blade, fixed by vertical bars at either end of it to a heavy frame, which sometimes bore the weight of the driver. Its use was to clean the surface of land after beans and such crops as leave it in a rough state, and also for cutting up weeds in the fallows.

There are two primitive implements, if they can be called such, which are not to be found named in any maker's list and yet are very useful on some farms. The first of these is the furrow-stone, which is simply a long smooth stone with a hole bored through it, which is drawn down a furrow after the horse-hoe, to bank up the earth again. The other is a solid drag of heavy baulks of wood, fixed between two beams to overlap like steps, and drawn by three horses. After seed has been harrowed in, this is driven over the field, to flatten the ground and raise a dust over it; thus it performs the work of a roller. A heavy wooden door, with the driver standing on it, used to do this work.

ROLLERS

Wooden rollers are but seldom seen now; they are generally regarded as the least effective, though, to be sure, they can be heavily weighted with logs and stones. They are still used in the south of Dorset and Hampshire. Stone rollers are common in Scotland and Ireland, Cornwall, Devon and other stone districts. But the type that is used on most farms began to be invented at the beginning of last century. By that time convex or furrow-rollers were in use on some hilly farms, then concave ridge-rollers, made to follow the curvature of the ridges, began to be employed in Essex. Spiky rollers were also

tried, and in Norfolk drill-rollers, which left impressions
like those of a dibble, into which most of the seed would
be swept. The Cambridge, or jointed and fluted roller,
has become the standard type for rolling wheat, for this
has the great advantage of not rubbing or tearing the
ground when it is turned. Smooth ones are used for
grass.

Another invention of the early nineteenth century must
be mentioned here, the furrow-slice compressor, which
is used to consolidate the surface of a clover-ley or olland
(where a hay-crop has been taken), after it has been
ploughed up in the autumn. This is the best way of
preparing such land for seed; and drills and coulters have
been used on the same machine.

THE GROWING CROP

The old parish custom of "beating the bounds" at
Rogation-tide was anciently associated with the calling
of a blessing on the crops; and this is still done in one or
two places in Essex.

When a crop of winter wheat seems too forward in
March or April, some farmers have recourse to what
would seem a very violent expedient; the field is folded
off and sheep put in to feed off the young shoots. They
leave the field to all appearance ruined, but before long
a fresh and vigorous growth takes place and the crop,
having been as it were pruned and manured in the spring,
is all the better and heavier for it. Sometimes it is
mown instead.

With the introduction of dibbling and drill-husbandry,
hoeing between the rows of growing corn became one
of the farmer's most important cares. Mention has been
made of horse-hoes, which, in Tull's system, accom-

panied his other invention of seed-drills, but these were intended to be used where the crop was grown on ridges a foot or more apart. Where the rows were closer together, though they might be scarified in March without risk of injury, this would not do when the crop had advanced further. A month later it was hand-hoed, four-inch hoes being used for barley, four-inch or six-inch for wheat. Finally, in May or early June, it was weeded or "thistled" by hand. Even this did not satisfy the careful farmers in Norfolk, for they would sometimes send women into the field when it was nearly ripe, if it were a field of red wheat, to pick off all the white ears which had grown with it, so that their sample might be unmixed.

Wheat is now seldom or never hoed by hand. Very much casual labour was employed by farmers in this work, but the dole has made it more difficult to obtain; and, like most other jobs, it can be done very well or very badly, and it is not easy to get it done well. The oldest form of hoe is a light square blade with a bent iron socket, but in the early part of last century the use of heavier hoes became general. A great variety of hoes was made, single ones with blades varying from an inch and a half to eight inches in width, "Portuguese hoes" with a point at each side and an angle between, triangular hoes and some with two or even three broad blades, besides several sorts of mattocks.

The farmer has many kinds of weeds to contend with, and hoeing was, short of pulling up by the roots, the best way of dealing with most of them. On some chalky lands, where poppies were very troublesome, hogs used in the early spring to be turned into the young corn; it was said that these animals were so fond of poppies that they would eat them and leave the wheat. Besides these there are charlock (cadlock or kilk, as it is locally called), bindweed and cockle, which strangle the growth of the crop, darnel or droke and shepherd's-needle, the seeds of which, by the old winnowing machinery, were not easily separated from the corn and lessened the value of the sample; crowfoot, coltsfoot and rattle. One of the most pestilent things is couch-grass, also called squitch, and in Cornwall stroyle. The term includes several perennial grasses whose roots grow so rankly that the ground is sometimes matted with them; and besides choking all other growth, they harbour grubs and other harmful insects. It can only be exterminated with rakes, heavy harrows, or cultivators, and burning; though it was in some places pared off and in others mixed with lime and made into compost with soil.

Thistles and docks are generally the worst enemies of all. The former are cut with scythes in the pastures, before the seed is formed, the latter must be rooted up; and here may be mentioned another tool which is now seldom seen (though gardeners use a small variety of it), namely the dock-grubber, with a forked point and a piece curled behind it to act as fulcrum: it was the farmer's constant companion on his walks.

Chapter VIII

MOWING WITH SCYTHES

IN a few places one may still occasionally see mowers
following one another across a field, mowing the
grass, oats or barley with scythes and moving in an
oblique row, like a flight of birds. Twenty years ago to
see ten or a dozen men at this work was no uncommon
thing; now it is rare to see more than two or three,
working in out-of-the-way corners or harvesting a crop
that has been laid by the rain. The leading scytheman
used quite generally to be called the "lord", to encourage him, as Ellis[1] says, to set a good pace to the
others and so to get the work done quickly, for they must
all keep up with him.

It is not very hard to handle a scythe after a fashion,
but there is great skill in using it well. A feeble old
man who is master of it will do better work, and with
less effort, than the most athletic novice; nor is it easy
for a hand which is accustomed to one type of scythe to
adapt itself to another.

The parts of a scythe are: the steel blade, the curved
wooden pole, called variously the batt, sneath, snead,
snath, etc.; the two nibs, hand-pins or doles; and the
grass-nail, a thin iron rod or stout wire, which connects
the blade and snath in front, and prevents the angle
between them from being choked with mowings.

The snath is often somewhat heavier at the base than
above and has usually a wide curve in the middle,
straightening out or with slight reflex curves above and
below; but it takes many forms, from a straight pole
with only one nib, or with a long curved lower one, to

[1] Author of *The Modern Husbandman* (1732–5).

an incredibly crooked piece of timber, cut out of the copse or hedge according to the user's fancy. Many old scythemen in the West of England would scorn to buy a ready-made snath which had been steamed and bent into a standard pattern; but despite this the manufacturers of such articles are obliged to keep a large number of different forms in stock.

The blade and nibs of a scythe can be adjusted or "set". By knocking out the pegs from the rings which secure them to the snath, the nibs can be turned round, raised or lowered; but the blade can only be turned outwards or inwards, so as to cut a wide or narrow swath. To alter the angle of the blade to the snath is called "tackling" the scythe, and to do this (as is necessary with a new scythe) is reckoned to be a blacksmith's job, as it involves heating and bending the tang, "tack" or "cray" which is welded to the blade.

There are several ways of setting a scythe, so that the distances between its parts shall be proportioned to the stature of the user. First, the heel of the snath is set against the right shoulder, and the lower nib set exactly at arm's length. The upper nib is then fixed at the length of the forearm (elbow to last joint of fingers) from the lower. The scythe is now laid across the left shoulder; the left hand grasping the upper nib and the lower nib resting against the left cheek, the heel of the scythe being behind the head. The right arm is then extended, and the point of the blade should come to the root of the thumb. This seems the most thorough way of measuring; but as a rule the scytheman simply holds the scythe with both nibs at arm's length, the snath being pressed against his groin, and then extends his right foot; the point of the blade should come "to the third lace-hole". Others again set the scythe upright beside them, its butt upon

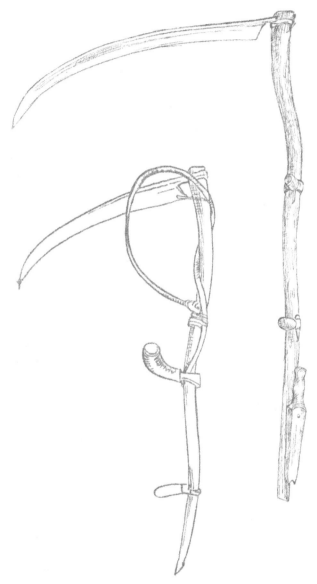

Scythe with "bow"   Scythe with ripe-stick
                           (Elan Valley, Wales)

Scythe for use with "crooks"

the ground by the heel of the right foot, and extend the
left one with the toe pointing out: the tip of the blade
should just clear it.

For sharpening, the "rubber" or "brittle-bat" is
carried in a loop behind the mower's belt. In Wales,
instead of a stone, a wooden "ripe-stick" (strick, in

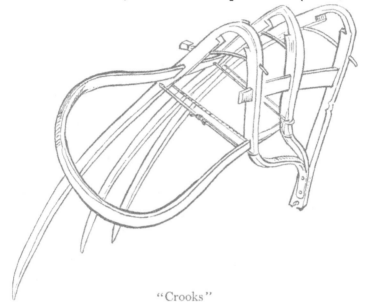

"Crooks"

Welsh) is used to whet the blade; it is made of oak and
square in section, and is smeared with grease and sanded,
the grease and sand being carried in cows' horns. This
ripe-stick is fixed on the upper end of the snath and serves
as a counterpoise to the blade.

The length of the cut made by a single sweep of the
scythe varies with the stature and reach of the mower,
its depth with the width of the angle at which the blade
is set. For thick grass the point must be turned well in,
so as to cut a narrow swath; with thin grass the angle
may be wider, for oats widest of all. Owing to the curve

of the scythe-blade the cut is widest about two-thirds across, to the left of the middle. In North Wales the average length, in mowing grass, is ten feet six inches, and the depth about one foot. In Cumberland, where the mowers move forward less rapidly, the cut is sometimes as much as twelve feet across.

Grass is left to lie in swaths just as it is cut, but when oats or barley are mowed with the scythe, a cradle or bow is attached to it, to collect the corn and lay it neatly together at the end of each sweep.

The cradle, also called creet or crooks, is hardly ever seen now; though efficient, it was thought too heavy, and troublesome to make. It was a light framework of wood, with several long prongs curved parallel to the scythe-blade, and was fixed to the sneath with a nail and tied with wire or string to the blade, which is perforated with one or two holes for this purpose. A less elaborate contrivance is sometimes seen in the western counties, called rods, consisting simply of a couple of curved sticks; one joining the snath to the hole in the blade, and the other joining the middle of this to the base of the blade. But the commonest attachment—though this, too, is not so often seen now—is a plain bow or bale made of a single hazel-rod twisted round the snath and brought back to a point some way under the lower nib. In East Anglia a "poker" used often to be added to this for oats; it was no more than a light, straight rod, fixed under the left nib and over the right one.

Before leaving the subject of scythes, it should be mentioned that there are, besides the ordinary ones, several special sorts: one with a short broad blade, for cutting furze and brambles, and another with a straight pole and single nib, sometimes used to clear ditches by the roadside and hence called a "roaden scythe".

HAYMAKING

The following description of haymaking by hand in North Devon is written down from a conversation with Mr Bawden of South Molton.

First, in the early morning, the men go out with scythes, the leading man cutting a swath straight along the side of the field, the next following him and cutting the next swath, and so on as it were in steps. The swaths are cut in one direction right across the field and back, not round and round as a reaping-machine cuts it.

Next, when the sun is on it, about nine o'clock, the swaths are thrown about with picks (pitchforks) by women and children and by the men when they have done mowing; thus they are thoroughly spread and partly dried.

The next business is rake-rolling. Small wooden hand-rakes are used to take the hay clear off the ground in little rolls, called rake-rolls. This is done so that all the "locks" (or thick lower grasses) shall be pulled up as high as possible so that the wind may blow through them. These rolls are "drowed" (thrown) about again with picks, and if not thoroughly dry, turned again.

If the weather is inclined to be wet, the hay is collected in the evening in rolls and heaped up, or "pooked" (in Devon a pook of hay is a haycock), as neatly as possible, so that the rain shall not penetrate.

The weather being clear in the morning, and likely to be fine for the day, these pooks of hay are thrown over the field, not spread thinly, but covering about half the ground, and turned with picks as much as may be needed to get the hay into good condition.

When the hay is fit to carry, it is "spurred in" to a windrow and thence loaded into the waggon by two men with picks working one on either side of the windrow and lifting it to the man who makes and treads the load. This load treader must be a practical chap, able to judge the balance of the load nicely.

In order to illustrate the diversity of local procedure in haymaking, I quote from Ellis' *Modern Husbandman*.

"Our common method in Hertfordshire is this; about eight o'clock, or sooner, the same morning the grass is mown, we ted or throw it out as fine as possible... The same day... it may be turned once or twice, and after that raked into wind-rows, and then put into grass-cocks. The second day we shake it into square leets... then put it into bastard-cocks, that are as big again. The third day we cock it up into heaps... the fourth day we put it into staddles, load it, and carry it away into a barn, cock, or stack."

Besides such variety of method as is simply a matter of local custom, there are many differences which are necessitated by the season of ripening or the condition of the crop in mountainous or marshy districts where it is difficult to use machines. Thus, on steep or boggy lands the old ways of mowing and haymaking survive of necessity—though farmers now, except the few small ones who with the help of their families can do all their own work, cannot afford the time and labour which is necessary for making hay well. Too often it is done carelessly and much too quickly.

In Devon the ricks are square; two men pitch up the hay and two work on the rick, one to take it in from the pitchers and one to spread it and make the rick. The rick-maker is the genius of the harvest field. When loading up the rick (if it is a square one) the hay ought to be passed to the rick-maker at the middle of the sides, not at the corners. He must have these clear and be able to

Rick-making, near Ashwick, Glos, 12 July 1930

see to make them himself, otherwise the rick will be
made "on the screw" and look unsightly and be unstable
when cut. After it has reached a certain height the hay
can no longer be passed up straight from the ground; a
waggon half-full of hay must be brought and a man must
stand on it to pass up the load to the man on the rick.
Another plan is for a ladder to be placed against the
rick, and a man to stand on it, with his back to it, four
or five rungs up, and for him to receive and pass up the
load of hay. The last half-load is piled up to make the ridge.

Horse elevators are certainly great savers of time and
trouble at this stage, which is otherwise the most tedious
of all and generally comes too at a time when the day's
work is drawing to an end and the men getting tired.

A generation ago rakes and pikes (or spekes) were
the only tools used in making hay, and it is said that in
Wiltshire it was loaded from the cocks on to the waggon
by hand without any tools, and that within the memory
of my informant. The old hay waggons, of the flat-
bottomed, hoop-raved type, would hold a deal of hay,
but it had to be loaded up with skill and judgment, so as
gradually to overhang and bow round the sides, somewhat like a loaf of bread baked in a tin. Names were
given to the corners of the waggon, "right quarter-
forward" and so on; the loader would call out these
names as he wished to have the hay passed up to him.
This was merely to carry it to the rick. The man or men
who made the rick did so generally upon some sort
of foundation: brushwood, faggots, harrows, old cart-
wheels or the like, the staddles being kept for cornstacks.
It was their special care to make it higher in the middle
at first, so that the hay might slope downwards from the
centre all round and thus not allow the rain, beating
against the sides of the haystack, to soak in and rot it.

During the last twenty years more and more engines, increasingly formidable, have invaded the hayfields— mowing-machines, swath-turners and tedders, side-delivery rakes, collecting-rakes, of every sort; followed by elevators driven first by horses and then by motors; loaders and even stackers—these last to supersede the brand-new machine-driven elevators. They have made haymaking seem a thing to be hurried through somehow; one of many noisy and dusty jobs to be over as soon as possible, instead of an immensely laborious, deliberate ritual, which must at all costs be done well in every detail, or the hay will be spoiled. It would have been a torment to a farmer of the old school to know that, through his own neglect or that of his men, his hay was in worse condition than it might have been.

One of the older inventions for carrying hay, not from cocks but from the cart-rows of rakings after the cocks have been carried, is the sweep, "tumbling-Jack" or "tumble-down-Dick", as it is called in the West. There are several forms of this; the most usual one is a beam with spikes sticking out from it before and behind, and drawn by two wires, with a boy behind to guide it. The spikes slide beneath the hay and collect it. When it is full it is drawn round to the rick, and there the driver presses down the handles so as to push the front spikes into the ground; the machine thus turns a somersault, leaving the pile of hay behind, and is ready to go forward empty for the next load. It must be owned that the use of these machines in unskilful hands is fraught with some risk to the horse's legs.

It may surprise some people to know that more hay-making is done by hand at present in Kent and Essex, and indeed within a score of miles from London, than in all the western counties together.

Chapter IX

HARVESTING IN THE OLD STYLE

IN most parts of England reaping with sickles has been given up since about 1870, but this work is still to be seen in some parts of Scotland and Ireland. The sickle is a distinct tool from the broad and smooth-edged fagging-hook, which is still used for many jobs and for a time took its place in the harvest-fields of most parts of England before reaping-machines became common. Its blade is in the form of a continuous curve, ending in a point several inches beyond the line of the handle; this point is not sharpened and serves to divide the straws of the standing corn. An inch or so from the point the edge is sharp and serrated, nicks being filed along the under side of the blade (which is somewhat concave), in such a way that they radiate, as it were, from the "heel" of the blade. About half a dozen patterns of sickle are still made, or at any rate listed by the large firms of tool-makers in Sheffield; those which still survive are mostly coarser-toothed and rather smaller than the sickles which were formerly used in England. It may be added that the sickle is used in May on the coast of Kerry, and perhaps by crofters and islanders on other rocky shores, for cutting the kelp or seaweed harvest, which is then at its best for turning into manure.

In reaping corn, the reaper stoops to his work or kneels on one knee, and leaning forward grasps in his left hand the straw near the ground, pushes the blade of the sickle round it and draws it towards him, pushing his left hand over it at the same time, to avoid the cut. After each cut he raises his left hand to clear the ears from those of the next handful to be reaped; and when he can

Reaping with the sickle (Rathcoursey, Co. Cork)

hold no more he lays out the bunch to his side, lifting it high over the standing corn with the ears supported in the curve of his sickle. As he works across the field he clears a strip about six feet wide (or less perhaps if the crop is heavy), reaping across the end of the strip from the outside to the inside and laying out his handfuls together in sheaves, ready for the binder.

A woman or girl generally does the binding. She must first shake out all grass and weeds from the straw and then, pulling out a handful from the bottom of the sheaf, she first twists it below the heads, turning it over so that they are held against the sheaf under the twist; and then dividing the bond she passes the two ends of it round the sheaf, again twisting them together and pushing them tightly under the bond. This, at any rate, is a common way of binding sheaves, but there are other sheaf-knots, which can be more conveniently described later.

Towards the end of the day the reapers put down their sickles and assist the binders in setting up the sheaves to dry in stooks or shocks. One binder is sufficient for three reapers, sometimes for more; and it used to be customary in some places for the children also to follow the reapers, making "lock-bonds" and laying the sheaves in them ready to be tied.

Nowadays reaping with sickles is almost entirely confined to small holdings, or small farms in districts which are full of large immovable stones, which make the use of machines impracticable. In such places two or three reapers, or a labourer and his family, are as many as will be seen working together; but when the sickle was the only means of harvesting all the corn that was grown, the farmer who had a large crop had to employ as many reapers as possible, in order to get the work finished before the corn was over-ripe. Where labour was cheap, the work was sometimes done with surprising speed. An old farmer in Ireland remembered seeing a wheat-field of fifty-five acres, in which no fewer than forty men were reaping with sickles, and women binding. On his going to look at the work, which was being beautifully done, he found two of the women fighting tooth and nail, tearing out one another's hair; the owner of the field was for letting them fight it out, but being a man of authority he intervened and stopped the battle.

In different districts there were various ways of arranging for the reaping to be done, and in some places it was customary for a band of harvesters to consist of a fixed number of men. In Northumberland six reapers were called a bandwin; in Yorkshire three shearers went out with one binder and the four were spoken of as a yan; but these terms are long since obsolete. In Cambridgeshire reapers worked in twos, the first making a lock-bond and laying in half the "shoof", the second filling it and tying it. The leader was generally called the lord or headman. In some counties it was his duty to call the others up by blowing a horn in the morning, and he would blow it again as a signal to cease work for meals and at the end of the day. In parts of Essex the custom of sounding the harvest-horn was kept up till 1914.

Sometimes the harvesters worked in families, and the farmer would then apportion each family's work by tying a knot at intervals in the standing corn.

The Irish reapers cut the straw close by the ground, and very little is wasted. This, though a slow process, leaves the field very neat and tidy; the ground is un-trampled, the sheaves free from weeds and the straw straight and unbroken for the thatcher's use. But in

8-2

England the stubble was left eight or ten inches long; and later in the year it was burnt to manure the land or "hammered off" with a scythe to use as litter for cattle. In Essex the stubble was generally left till after Christmas as cover for the partridges; then it was cut off and used for making lambing-pens or for fuel.

A skilful and laborious man may reap a half-acre in a day. Formerly men worked for long hours throughout the harvest; and there are labourers still working in Somerset and Gloucestershire who have many times been up all night reaping by moonlight. One of them affirms that he and another man between them in one season mowed and reaped, of hay and corn, not less than two hundred acres of land. To sustain them in their Herculean labours a vast deal of fuel was needed. A gallon of cider to each man, and often ale in addition, was the regular daily allowance while this work lasted. The drink was carried in a wooden bottle like a little tub, slung at the belt; with a cork and an air stop which had to be removed before drinking from it. Every morning these were filled up by the farmer's wife and stood in a row outside the kitchen, one for each man. A farm near Bishop's Lydeard still continues the custom; perhaps others do also, but the farm labourer of to-day drinks very much less than his forefathers, for his work is no longer so constant and severe as to make it necessary.

Many farmers gave their men a meat dinner once a week, sometimes twice. The other meals during harvest were breakfast, elevenses, dinner and fourses—in some places elevenses was called "beaver" or "cheesing"—but there was a good deal of difference in the local significations of these terms and the times at which the meals were eaten. Meals at harvesting were generally somewhat different from those at other times. The school children had a holiday at harvest-time; in Norfolk the girls went out "carrying elevenses" and "carrying fourses", and the boys, whose duty it was to lead the horses which drew the harvest-waggons were said to be busied in "hollering holdyer"; this was a signal to the men on top of the load to hold tight when the waggon moved on, and was yelled so loudly as to be heard, if possible, not only in the next parish, but in the next county too!

In different counties there were many ways of setting up shocks or stooks to dry before they were ready to carry to the stack or the barn. In wet districts, as soon as may be, the stooks are put into larger heaps called mows, the better to protect the corn from the wet.

The number of sheaves in the shock varies in different districts; formerly it was regularly fixed, but nowadays the terms shock or stook are loosely used by most farmers, and probably not many harvesters trouble themselves in the least about how many sheaves they set up, beyond the fact that too few are liable to be blown down, and too many will not dry easily. The stooks are made in straight lines down the field; the harvester holding a couple of sheaves by the heads, one under each arm, and dropping their butts on the ground at either side of his feet: so that the two rest upright against one another. More pairs of sheaves are generally added behind and before, so that the finished stook contains six, eight, ten or even twelve sheaves. It is a mistake to place an odd sheaf at the end, for this prevents the air from circulating through the corn and drying it. Formerly a "shock" was generally understood to contain six sheaves and a stook, stowk or hattock, twelve sheaves; in the northern counties (Derbyshire, Yorkshire, Cheshire, and West-morland), twenty-four sheaves, that is, four shocks or two stooks, made up a threave, which was a convenient measure in those districts. In Cumberland, however, ten sheaves were reckoned to a hattock, or twelve to a stook. The term threave, thrave or trace was a pretty general one in several of the southern counties also, though it has now dropped out of common use. Where the land was ploughed in ten-foot stitches in Essex, the sheaves were set up in every alternate furrow, so that the rows of stooks, or "traves" as they were there called, stood at the breadth of two ridges apart from one another.

In the south-western counties, except Cornwall, stooks were made to contain ten sheaves, originally, it is said, for convenience in paying tithes when they were collected in kind; hence they are sometimes called tethins or teddings. The collecting of tithes in kind was commuted for money payment by Act of Parliament in 1826, and it is somewhat startling to find that it may still be no further off than a second-hand tradition. Last haymaking season an old Wiltshire labourer, who is still hard at work at eighty-four, beguiled the dinner-hour by telling stories which he had heard when a boy from an old man with whom he then worked. This man had explained to him how at harvest-time it had been his duty to carry round green boughs and lay one on every tenth stook, which was thus set apart for the parson. The farmer first carried his own sheaves, then the rector's waggon would follow and pick up all his, carrying them off to the tithe barn. This old labourer had several stories about tithing, always at the expense of the parson. A certain very mean and grasping rector called on one of his parishioners, a poor widow with a large family, having heard that her sow had farrowed and intending to claim the tenth pig of the litter. For some time she argued the point, but he was firm and not to be put to shame. At last she said, "Well zur, if you do have the tenth pig then you do take the tenth child too, for I've got eleven o' they!" Whether the rector agreed to these terms is not related. The same parson had an argument with another of his parishioners on the subject of bees, claiming the tenth swarm of the season. In the end the bee-keeper entered his study one day with a skep in his hand, turned it upside down and shook out all the bees, exclaiming, "Here you be sir, the bees is yourn and the hive's mine!" He made good his retreat before the rector could collect his wits, let alone the bees.

In harvesting other crops than wheat, different methods had sometimes to be employed. When barley was bound in sheaves, on account of the shortness of its straw, it had to be tied with double or lock-bonds, the binder fastening two small handfuls together by the ears and tying the tails the other side. In Essex and parts of Norfolk, and elsewhere, it was not bound at all, but being mown with scythe and cradle, was laid out in rows; and when the sun had been on these for some time, they were turned over with long three-pronged pitchforks, called barley-forks, so that the other sides should be dried also, and then carried loose in the waggon. It was a good plan, despite its seeming awkwardness, for barley is more easily injured by rain at harvest than any other crop, and it dries much more quickly loose than in sheaves.

In Kent barley used to be made into mows, and this was called haling. Four sheaves were placed together two against two, their ears all together and butts outward, then four more on these with their butts somewhat off the ground; a third tier likewise, and finally three sheaves fastened together, with ears downwards so as to make a covering over the top. Thus the whole mow contained fifteen sheaves. Something much like this is done in Cardiganshire, where the stooks consist of four sheaves only. The mows are made by setting about fifteen more sheaves round a stook, their butts also on the ground; then another fifteen (or perhaps fewer) in a second and third tier; lastly three or four sheaves are tied close together at the top to keep out the wet. In Pembrokeshire wheat is sometimes thus made into mows, but not oats. In Co. Galway, where a good deal of reaping is done with sickles and the sheaves are very small, they are laid into "barts", which contain thirty sheaves of wheat or twenty of oats. In other parts of the country, on account of the frequent rains at harvesting-time, the stooks are often made into mows as soon as the corn is dry enough to allow this.

Farmers used to leave their corn longer to dry in stooks than they commonly do now. Sometimes the reaping took a month, and when the corn was all stooked and finished—it might be on a Wednesday or Thursday —they would take another day or so to lay the rick foundations; and then on Saturday the farmer would very likely give his men a holiday and not begin stacking till Monday. But now corn may be cut, stacked, threshed and sent to the mill, all in a fortnight.

There were several old customs at harvesting, some local, others widespread, but all more or less of a ritual-istic nature. In Devonshire, before a field was reaped, the farmer's wife was known to step in, before she would allow the reapers to begin, and cut the first few handfuls with her own hand, "for the church"; these she would afterwards make into little sheaves and lay upon the altar. This was perhaps a pretty fancy of her own; but the other customs were possibly of pagan origin and had to do with the last sheaves cut. One of these was the bringing in of the "neck", which was made of the last handful cut, the man who cut it standing between two sickles laid edge to edge on the ground and crying "I have a neck!" There were sometimes set responses from the other reapers and in the end a race to take it into the barn. The last load to be brought in, called the "horkey load", was the centre of great rejoicing; it was crowned with a green bough and sometimes with a "harvest-home sheaf" of great size, and the men, women and children rode home on it shouting and cheering. The great sheaf had to go at the bottom or in the middle of the rick and the bough was sometimes set on the top.

In Essex they went round to the farm or manor and "hollered largess", which the master gave them in kind; one giving a barrel of beer or cider, another giving meat or bacon, and so on. In some places they levied contributions from the shopkeepers of the nearest market-town or hamlet. Then they would join forces and have the horkey or harvest-supper, it might be in a public-house, but more often in a barn. This giving of largess was gradually replaced by gifts of money, and in some places the harvest supper was paid for by the farmer, especially if he were a well-to-do man. This was of course besides the two or three meat dinners a week which many farmers gave their harvesters. At the horkeys a few old songs, and probably more new ones, were sung, and in former years one or two old men would perform country-dances on a board. But since the passing of the Agricultural Wages Bill, the horkey has been generally abandoned, though one or two landowners in the eastern counties are still generous enough to give a supper each year.

HARVESTING: LATER DEVELOPMENTS

It has already been said that sickles were in many places succeeded by fagging-hooks, some sixty or seventy years ago. The latter tools have a larger and less curved blade, without serrations and not pointed, but with a square or slanted end. They do not therefore saw through the straw, but slash it, a larger quantity being cut at one blow. So the work was done quickly, but rather roughly, and "taking-out", or laying the corn in sheaves for the binder, was less easy. The man who reaped with a fagging-hook, instead of grasping the corn in his left hand, would draw it towards him with a short wooden crook.

The fagging-hook is sometimes used in the bean-fields, but beans are harvested in other ways also. If they grow up well, they may be cut with the reaping machine; in a backward year, when they "kid" or form pods near the ground, in Gloucestershire they are pulled by hand, for the roots do not strike deep and the plants come up easily.

There are some peculiar things in the harvesting of beans, which, though they are extremely beautiful and sweet-scented when in flower, are a somewhat unsightly and untidy crop when ripe. They cannot be tied with their own bine without breaking off some of the pods and scattering the contents, and so, where they are grown in Kent, bonds of twisted oat-straw are carried into the field to bind them. They are left in stooks long enough to dry the haulm, which if too green may turn them mouldy, and they are threshed as soon as possible after they have been brought in. The haulm makes good litter and when fresh can be used for feeding cattle. In the fen districts beans are sometimes harvested with hooks, pointed like sickles, but smaller and smooth edged. These are also used for cutting turnip- and mustard-seed, which is grown there in large quantities. Near Southend in Essex mustard used to be drilled in rows a foot apart, and the plants are said to have grown up eight feet high, their stems as thick as one's wrist and branching like trees; and when they were reaped, by women with sickles, they were found to be full of old birds' nests.

Peas are cut with a tool which is called a pea-swap in Kent; this is held in the right hand and a wooden crook in the other. It is like a small scythe, with a short straight blade projecting at right angles to the pole or snath, which is also straight and about four feet long, with a loop at the top through which the right forearm is thrust and a nib which projects half-way down, for the hand to grasp.

The scythe is used nearly everywhere for clearing a way round the edge of a field for the horses and machine and sometimes for mowing the whole crop in a wet season when it is beaten down by the wind and rain; it is also the usual means of cutting oats in many mountainous districts. Sometimes where the crop is battered one or two labourers go in front of the reaping-machine raising the straw with pitchforks, but much time is wasted, for the machine can only cut efficiently against the direction towards which the straw is laid. The scytheman, too, in working round such a field, when he comes to a side from which the wind has blown, will take it in strips of twenty or thirty yards at a time, working back to the "layer-out" who collects the oats into sheaves and the binder who follows him. A bale is often fixed to the scythe blade and snath, as has been described above.

Reaping machines developed slowly during the first half of the nineteenth century, and it was not till the third quarter of it that they began to be used by farmers throughout the country. At first they were clumsy and frequently broke down, the knives every now and then becoming choked and immovable, to the constant delay of the work and the exasperation of all who had to do with them. Moreover the accommodation for such machines is none too good on most farms and they must take their chance for eleven months of the year in an open cart-house, which is the roosting-place of all the farmyard poultry, where they may be damaged by the wheels of waggons or by having thrown on top of them miscellaneous items of ironmongery, harrows, rakes, pitchforks, ploughshares, fruit-baskets, and bags of lime. It is not surprising that a thorough cleaning and a few repairs are often needed at the beginning of the season. But the reaper-and-binder machines which are generally in use now, made by firms of good repute, are amazingly strong and efficient, considering the necessary intricacy of their parts and the rough treatment they generally get.

The first reaping machines, made in the early nineteenth century, went *in front* of the horses, which were harnessed to a long pole behind; thus it was not necessary to clear round a field before putting the machines in. The first to be at all generally adopted was McCormick's. At Gringham, near Bawtry, there is said to have been one which was propelled by four bulls, which were also used for ploughing. But of those which first became common, two types are still sometimes to be seen. One of these is Bamlett's "sailer", which is used still in Lincolnshire and Norfolk, because it is lighter in draught and therefore more suitable for soft land than the self-binder which has generally replaced it in other parts of the country.

This is drawn by three horses, two being harnessed abreast to the pole and a boy riding the leader. The other is the side-delivery reaper, which has two seats, one for the driver and a somewhat lower one for a boy, whose business it is to push the corn off the "sheafing-table" on which it falls, by means of a wooden rake, which is made for the purpose, with a head fixed slantwise into a long handle.

When these machines first came in, they immediately reduced the necessary number of harvesters, but they did not by any means lighten the work for those who were engaged in it. The sheaves still had to be bound by hand, and the constant noise and hurry of the machine and the need for the binders to keep pace with it and to move the sheaves out of its path imposed a greater strain upon them and took away much of the pleasure and satisfaction which there had hitherto been in this always hard and trying work. A woman of more than ordinary strength and endurance told how she had followed one of the old reaping-machines all day from eight in the morning, binding sheaves at the rate of eighteen for every round of the machine. At eight in the evening the machine broke down, and she fainted over the sheaf she was tying.

The early reaper-and-binder machines tied the sheaves with wire, but this, when accidentally cut with the chaff, was found to be injurious both to the chaff-cutter and the cattle; and the invention of the twine binder was a great step forward. The far-reaching effects of this use of twine must be considered in the following section.

SHEAF-KNOTS

Sheaves are nowadays nearly always tied by the self-binder with twine, which is automatically cut and thrown out by the threshing-machine, but the old way of binding by hand is still to be seen when the edges of a field are being cleared with scythes. It is by no means easy to tie a knot neatly and effectually in straw, and the younger generation of labourers are often impatient of the intractability of the stuff and prefer, when they can, to provide themselves with pieces of twine. Their fathers and mothers, having learnt the old sheaf-knots almost in

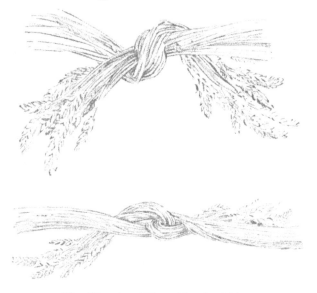

Sheaf-knots: Offley, Hertfordshire

infancy, tie them with inimitable rapidity and deftness, though they are often unable to do it deliberately or in material other than straw and are nearly always totally incapable of explaining the process in words. Indeed a verbal description of a knot is necessarily clumsy and obscure; the illustrations must serve to show the construction of some of them, though it is impossible to give a notion of the unconscious sleight-of-hand by which they are produced.

Sheaf-bonds are of two kinds; single, in which one length of straw spans the whole sheaf, the knot joining heads to butts; and double, in which two lengths are joined by the

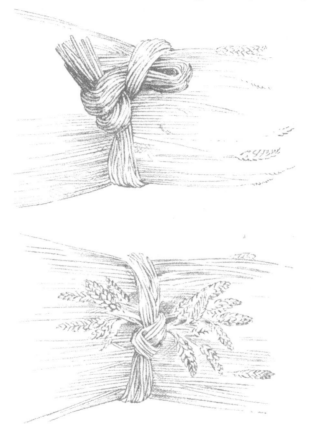

Sheaf-knots: Romney Marsh

heads, and their butts united on the other side of the sheaf. Single bonds are used when the sheaves are small, double or lock-bonds where the sheaves are large or the straw short. Some farmers insisted on small sheaves, because they dry quicker and better than large ones, and

would even cut lock-bonds wherever they found them
being made and have the sheaves tied again with single
ones.

It is really surprising to find how many kinds of bonds

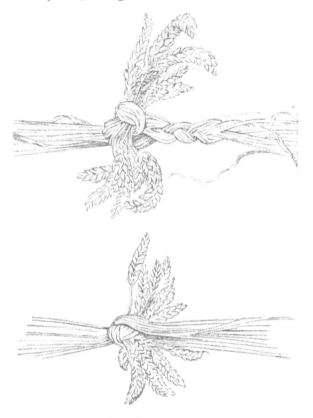

Sheaf-knots: Dorset

can be made with straw; for though in many districts
only two or three ways are generally practised, it is not
at all uncommon in Lincolnshire, where many labourers
from different parts of the country are employed, to see
half a dozen men binding sheaves in a field and each

making a different bond. Again, fastenings which, when made, look much alike, may be actually produced by various knacks or even on different principles.

One of the simplest forms of double bond has already

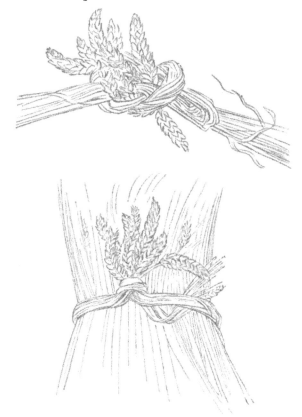

Sheaf-knots: Dorset

been described; it is most commonly used for binding oats. There are two distinct ways of twisting the heads so that they will hold. In the first a bunch of ears is placed upright on either side of the left index finger, then grasping them with the thumb and second finger of that

hand, the index finger is turned down, and they are
twisted and pushed over it and against the sheaf with the
right hand. The other way is to take the ears in a handful,
twist them round, then open the straw and bring it over
on either side, the ears being thus pressed against the
side of the sheaf. The two ends are then passed round,

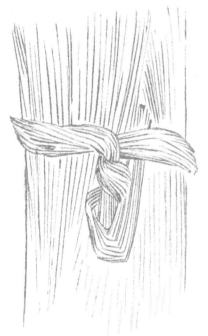

Reed-cutter's bond: Salhouse, Norfolk

the sheaf being reversed, and they are turned one round
the other and pushed under the bond, forming an "ordinary tuck".

In tying oats with a single bond the straw is sometimes twisted like a rope before it is put on, and this
greatly strengthens it. The ends are held in both hands
and a twist given, the left-hand end being then put under

the right armpit; the other end is now taken by the left hand and the bond again twisted and reversed; this is repeated very quickly and dexterously two or three times and for short bonds is as good as using a twister. The ends of these single bonds are often twisted round each other and tucked under—a fastening which in the north-eastern counties is called a wool-warp; in the southern counties it is more common to leave the heads standing up, a form sometimes called a "pump-handle". It is

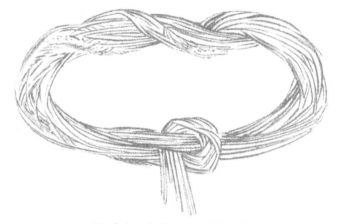

Rush-bond: Romney Marsh

scarcely necessary to add that such knots as are used for single bonds do equally well for uniting the tails of lock-bonds.

Wheat is much neater to handle than oats, and though it can be bound just as simply, more elaborate knots are often made where lock-bonds are used. One of these is a reef bow, which I have seen a Dorset labourer tie almost in one movement, without taking his fingers off the straw. Another is a simple slip knot, made by cross-ing the heads of two handfuls, bringing the stems of one across the neck of the other, dividing them, and passing one part over and one under the heads of the other. In some places this is called the "goose's neck"; it will come undone in the threshing machine or under the flail so that the ears are threshed out clean.

A more elaborate knot, similar to the last, was used in Dorset for tying bundles of reed. Two lengths of straw were crossed in a half-hitch, then one end was put over the other and divided in two, and finally braided up in three. It was done with amazingly little waste of time.

River-reed on account of its stiffness requires a different form of bond; those used in Norfolk and on Romney Marsh are illustrated.

It was an almost universal practice to bind sheaves, faggots, or almost any other growing thing that is cut and collected, with "its own bond"; that is to say, with a bond made of the same material. Besides wheat and oats, rye, buckwheat, flax and hemp were made into sheaves and tied thus, each with the twist or knot which belonged to the crop and the district. Hay, when made into trusses by hand and not with the hay-trussing machine, is tied with hay-bonds; bales of wool were fastened with a fleece to each bale, drawn out into a rope on a wimble; even teasels were tied into heads with the stem of a long one. Barley and beans were about the only exceptions to this rule. Faggots and thatching-spikes were tied in bundles with twisted withs of hazel or willow, and furze-faggots with brambles—which, by the way, are sometimes split and used for tying birch-besoms. But just as twine is used on nearly all sorts of sheaves, wire is beginning to be used to tie faggots, apparently for no better reason than that less skill is needed to fasten it, for it can scarcely be from any possibility of economy either in materials or labour.

GLEANING

From time immemorial the poorer people had a right to glean in the harvest-fields after the farmer had carried his sheaves, and by this means many families managed to keep themselves in bread throughout the winter. The custom survives in a very few parts of the country; ten or fifteen years ago it was much more common, but from several causes it is quickly becoming extinct. The chief reason is that there is no longer an urgent necessity for it; the labourer's wages are higher, it is no longer common for him to be in actual want, and so there is much less incentive to thrift. With the increase of his pay he has forfeited or relinquished his right to many of the perquisites which he had traditionally assumed for centuries in the past. There is also a very strong kind of pride—false pride perhaps—or a sense of social position, which deters many from claiming rights which are theirs by inheritance; and when some give them up, the rest soon follow for fear of being thought paupers. Besides, gleaning was work for the women and girls, and "you can't go gleaning in silk stockings!" But the introduction of reaping machines is the chief reason why there are no gleaners now. Reaping with fagging-hooks and scythes left more for the gleaners, if anything, than did sickles; but the earlier reaping-machines and horse-rakes left less behind them, the side-delivery reaper and the self-binder successively less and less, till there was not enough to be worth the toil of gleaning, and so the custom entirely died out.

After the field was raked one of the church bells was rung, at about eight in the morning and again at six in the evening, as a signal to the gleaners that they might be in the fields between those hours; and the women and

children were up early and would wait by the gate till
the bell was rung. In 1910 the gleaning bell was still
rung in twenty or thirty parishes in Essex; in 1931,
though there is still a little gleaning in several parishes,
this old custom survives only at Farnham in Essex. A
man was chosen to ring the bell and his name posted on
the church door; each family of gleaners paid him a fee
of twopence or sixpence for his services.

A stook or thrave of corn, called the "guard-sheaf",
was left near the gate until the farmer was ready to
admit the gleaners; when it was removed they might
enter and begin work. In Norfolk three sheaves, set up
together and known as the "policeman", answered the
same purpose; in Lincolnshire there was a contrary
custom of setting a white flag in the stubble as a signal
that the gleaners might enter. People who were known
to be honest and respectable had sometimes, by favour
of the farmer, the privilege of gleaning between the
thraves; much as Ruth had in the fields of Boaz. But
before the majority could enter the stubble was hand-
raked by men and boys, and these rakings made into
little sheaves and put with the thraves. After these were
carted the ground on which they had stood was likewise
raked for the farmer, and even then the gleaners found
more than they would find after the machine now. Where
the parish boundary crossed a field, there was sometimes
no little dissension between the gleaners of the two
parishes. Each family reckoned to gather so many handfuls a day, if possible, before they went home. Sometimes
they had a use for the straw, but more often they cut it
off about six inches below the ears and left it in the field.
They carried home the gleanings in large head-bundles,
or in sacks or perambulators.

What little gleanings are gathered now, mostly between Saffron Walden, Dunmow and Braintree, are used to feed chickens; the old windmills which ground the corn and dressed the flour being done away with, and little or no bread baked at home.

An Essex labourer described how a man who had a hand-threshing machine used to thresh out the corn for them at night, but sometimes it would be beaten out at home with flails. A miller, Metson of Sible Hedingham, used to grind the gleaners' corn, but it was necessary to wait for a wind. The usual arrangement was that he kept the bran as payment for the trouble of grinding, the cost of grinding and dressing being alternatively eightpence a bushel. The miller, to avoid confusion, numbered each family's gleanings in a separate bag.

The mother of each family used to bake once a week in the summer and once a fortnight in winter; and the bread, though rather dark, was better after ten days than white baker's-bread after two. Sometimes she would be up early and make "apple-cake" or "huffers" for the children's breakfast.

At that time every labourer's cottage had its own oven, and the wheat stubble or "harme" was often the men's perquisite after the shooting season. The farmer lent his cart for carrying it, and it was made into stacks for heating the baking ovens, being pulled out from the stack with a "harme-hook", or barbed spear, such as is still used in Wales. Though wages were low, there were in most districts after-perquisites which made it possible for a family to get enough good food and fuel to live within their earnings. The rent for a cottage might be only ninepence or a shilling a week, milk threepence a quart, butter tenpence a pound; cider, cabbages and white turnips (where the farms produced them) were often given for nothing.

Chapter X

STACKING AND RICK-MAKING

HAYSTACKS and cornricks have an almost endless variety of form and fashion; in almost every place there is some local peculiarity. Much depends, of course, on the conditions under which the crop is harvested. In wet and mountainous places there is generally more difficulty in bringing it in safely and special care must be taken to shape it so as best to resist the constant soakings of mist and winter rain. In windy places the thatch must have special strength and tightness, in fertile and sheltered places the ricks must be large and capacious to save unnecessary thatching; sometimes stacks are even built on to one another like a row of houses in a street, but this makes them all the more liable to damage and is very doubtful economy. If the hay is at all damp, it is of course better to put it into small than large stacks.

Another reason for variety is that there are many different materials which can be used for thatching. Wheat-straw is most usual, but oat-straw, river-reed, meadow-rush, rye, and fern are used also, the choice depending on what is most economical in each district. The foundations of the rick are determined in the same way. If it is of hay, anything will do which will keep the damp from under it; faggots are best, but brushwood, hurdles, or old harrows and cart-wheels are very often used. In Romney Marsh the willow-shoots which are cut out of the dykes every year are made into bundles for this purpose; after they have remained there for a year they make excellent firing.

As is well known, haystacks are liable to catch fire or

"mow-burn" if the hay is stacked before it is properly
dry. An old way of preventing this was to build it round
a sack filled with straw and to draw up the sack by degrees, so as to leave a flue or vent in the middle of the
haystack. But there are two objections to this: if there
were no ventilation underneath the stack also, the hay
round the hole would turn mouldy, and if there were,
the draught through the stack might make it more liable
still to burn. Some farmers thrust a long stick into the
middle of each rick; which primitive thermometer is now
and then taken out and felt at the inward end to see
whether the heat is becoming dangerous. On the other
hand some farmers when stacking very dry and withered
hay which has been cut too late would sprinkle a few
thin layers of green mowings in the stack, to heat it
somewhat and "give it a flavour". This is a questionable
practice, but many farmers think that hay which is rather
brown contains more nourishment.

In stacking corn, it is most important to preserve it
from rats, mice and birds. Cornricks are nearly always
round or rounded at the ends, the sheaves being laid
with their heads inwards; but even so the sparrows will
sometimes manage to pull out single straws, one at a
time, and so one sees occasionally a sort of entanglement
fixed round the rick to deter them.

The old way is to build them on staddles, that is,
stone mushroom-shaped piers, with baulks of timber laid
across them, so that the rats shall not climb up. But
nowadays, when the corn does not remain so long in
the rick and the threshing-machine finishes all its work
in a day or two, this is not so necessary; and staddles
have several drawbacks. The space they occupy from the
ground up is equivalent to a load, or a load and a half,
and it is much more difficult to lay the bed of a rick on

the platform than near the ground and to balance it securely. For these reasons staddles are now to be seen on very few farms, and their use is almost unknown.

There were other inventions for the same purpose, but less effective. In many stone-wall countries, solid walled foundations were made, like large flat cheeses, and there were also inventions like low wooden tables or like the seats which used to be made round the trunks of old trees in gardens.

It may be worth while to describe some of the local styles of stacking and thatching, since with the greatly increasing use of iron haybarns these arts are becoming unnecessary and in some districts quite extinct. Moreover, good thatchers are not very common and few of them take pride enough in their work to add the ornamental finishes which were locally distinctive.

The shape and style of ricks is one of the most obviously noticeable features in each district to anyone who travels through the country. If one stops to examine them attentively the most surprising differences of principle become apparent. In Middlesex and most of the eastern counties the haystacks are oblong, high and gable-ended. In Kent the ends are generally sloped back to the ridge from a short distance down, in other southern counties rather more so, often from a point nearly as low as the side eaves. In Wiltshire the stacks incline to be squarer in plan, with only a short ridge, the eaves level all round; in Devon and parts of Somerset there is no ridge at all, but all four sides are alike and the thatch comes to a point. Elsewhere in Somerset, especially on the road from Bath to Chewton Mendip, small round haystacks are seen, very neatly shaped and raked; and for a distance of three feet from the ground they are closely sheared with a hayknife. This clipping would be likely to let the rain soak in and rot the hay at the bottom, were it not that it is sloped downwards and outwards from the middle of the stack and is overhung by that above, the circumference at the eaves being greater by several feet than that at the base.

There is a quite distinct system of thatching in Wales; here the thatch is fastened into position by a network of straw- or hay-bonds, the ricks being both round and oblong and varying greatly in proportions. On long ricks, double straw-bonds are often made to span the rick from side to side, while single bonds, sometimes of hay (which was the old method) but more often of straw or twine, are run through these, parallel to one another and from end to end of the rick. Some of the prettiest work of this kind is done in Anglesey. Thatching proceeds, as in England, from one end to the other of the rick, and as it does so the double bond is stretched over the thatch by a wooden pin which is moved down as the thatch progresses; at either side, near the base of the rick, the double bonds are tied to the hay. The thatch is made secure by the horizontal bonds, which are passed between the two strands of the straw-rope or else twisted round them. The way of tying the straw-rope to the haystack is simple and secure. The sides of the rick must have been carefully raked so that the hay holds firmly together; a larger bunch of it is then seized in one hand, while with the other the end of the straw-bond is stretched over it, the two are twisted together, and their end pushed under the stretched part. Thus the whole thatch is made fast without the use of any spars or wood save the short spike which is used as a tool in stretching the cross-bonds.

It should be added that while the typical shape of ricks in Anglesey is oblong in plan and rounded at shoulders and ends, the number and disposition of the bonds varies much, according to the defence which is needed against the prevailing wind. Few ricks are finished in the same way at both ends.

In other parts of North Wales the ricks are made on the same lines, though with less fancy. They are often longer in shape, rounded at the ends, and with the ridge bowed; the thatch does not come down to the end of the slope, where the eaves would otherwise be, and may cover no more than the ridge and two or three feet at either side. The long bonds are twisted and secured together on a stout wooden spike driven in at either end of the rick, pretty low down. The cross-bonds are usually fixed to single spars driven in to the sides with points directed upwards, their heads pressing the loop of the bond into the rick. These ridge-thatches are most often seen in mountainous places and are of oaten straw or rushes.

In Cheshire and Lancashire the style of thatching is somewhat like the Welsh, though twine seems to have quite superseded hay for the horizontal bonds, while for the stouter cross-bonds rope is often used instead of straw. But in these counties the ricks still have an English look, from their sharp ridges and general squareness of proportion.

In the poorer parts of Scotland and Ireland, and other wet mountainous districts where the hay is harvested with difficulty, the stack is generally made like a large round haycock, with a curved outline continuing from peak to base. The thatch is often at the top only, held on there by crossed bonds, weighted at both ends with stones, or with circumferent bonds added to form a net at the summit. On many there is no thatch; crofters by the sea use an old fishing-net, others ram the hay into position with stakes or baulks of timber. But these are the meanest sort of haystack, and since it is seldom worth their owners' while to put up haybarns, the species is in no danger of dying out.

Thatching Knaves (Blatherwyck, Northants)

RICK-ORNAMENTS

It used to be a fairly general custom to decorate ricks and stacks, or at least one of them in every rickyard, by way of completing the work of thatching with something of a flourish. One of the prettiest and probably oldest customs in Norfolk was to set an unthreshed sheaf of wheat on the top of the rick for the birds.

The very graceful finish which was called "crowning the rick" was generally done on the largest and finest wheatrick, but now only the simplest and slightest forms of ornament are seen, and even they are being gradually abandoned. Sometimes a rick is surmounted by a handful of threshed-out ears made fast with a straw-plait, and in districts where reed-thatching is practised a little sheaf or fascia of reeds answers the same purpose. In the West of England haystacks, too, were often surmounted by a straw figure in the shape of a cock or other bird, a cross, a boat, an apple or a turnip, which the Somerset folk call a "dolly". In Devon a cock was often set at each end of the rick.

The thatchers in Hertfordshire were experts in straw-plaiting and often spent the midday hour in weaving a bird round a piece of board, cut out to the required shape, and sometimes as much as three feet across, or on more elaborate fancies, such as toy windmills or pigeon-cotes. Sometimes they would make a working weather-cock, mounted on a stick which would revolve in the neck of a pint bottle embedded in the summit of the rick.

In Wales there are endless varieties of ornament. In Cardiganshire especially neighbouring farmers seem to vie with one another in inventing them and in combining them with different forms of thatch-fastening; now tying the thatch down, now holding it with pegs, now weighting it with stones. Some of the ricks are crested with a thin straw-bond twisted round a stick, some with a knob of thatch tied up at intervals, others with a twist of straw round a straight bundle, and occasionally even with a slice of turf, cut to fit beneath the topmost tying-bond. The ridges of long ricks are now and then finished with a double straw-rope, between the strands of which the ridge-ends of the thatch are pushed up in alternate handfuls; and in Radnorshire ricks were even made with a crenellation of doubled and twisted handfuls of thatch continuing from end to end.

"NECKS" OF STRAW, BUTTON-HOLES

This generation is so accustomed to ready-made ornaments, of no beauty whatever, that hand-made things begin to be objects of curiosity and the most trifling of

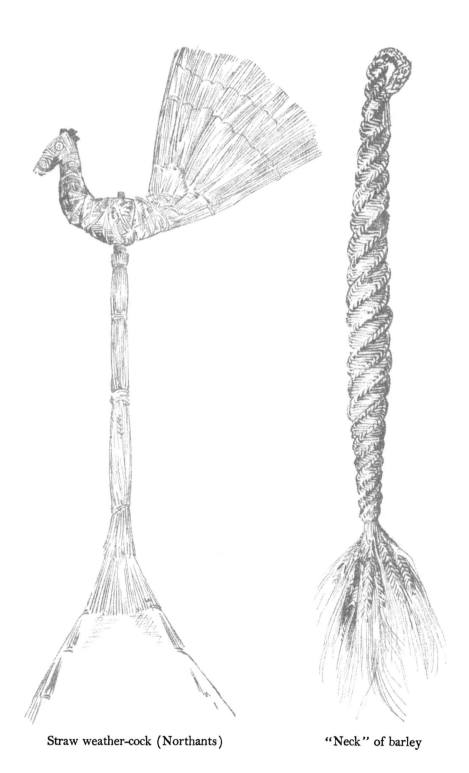

Straw weather-cock (Northants)   "Neck" of barley

them becomes worthy of serious notice. Our national schools undertake to teach children "hand-crafts" of one sort or another; but the old traditions of needlework, embroidery, weaving and plaiting have, despite some spirited revivalists, long since ceased to be a part of common life.

An object which used to be seen quite often in cottages was a long sheaf or bundle of corn, with an ornamental twisted covering; it was sometimes called a "neck". This may at one time have had a religious significance[1], but it has for long been made only, as country people say, "for a hobby"; either as a decoration for the harvest festival or to be hung up and admired in the village ale-house. Whether it was originally the "kern baby" or "neck of corn", made from the last sheaf reaped and kept till the following year to ensure the continuance of crops and seasons, is a matter for curious speculation. There are still a few people in Essex who can make them, and specimens are to be met with in Cambridge-shire, Northamptonshire, Bedfordshire and Hertford-shire and probably elsewhere, though the skill of making them is now nearly lost.

In these counties it is still common for small bits of straw, braided in twos or fives, to be stuck in boys' buttonholes or hats, but this class of home-made orna-ment has come to be disdained and with the march of education will no doubt soon be quite forgotten. A Northamptonshire button-hole is reproduced on the title-page.

[1] "Herodotus relates how sacred objects bound up in wheaten straw were brought from the Hyperboreans (of the Baltic) to the Scythians (of the lower Danube and South Russia), the latter for-warding them westward to the Adriatic."—British Museum Guide, *Early Iron Age*, p. 9.

STRAW-PLAIT: ESSEX, BEDFORDSHIRE AND HERTFORDSHIRE

Till lately wheat-straw was an important product of farms in Bedfordshire and Hertfordshire on account of the straw hat trade centred at Luton. The straw is exceptionally fine and bright in this district, nearly white in colour and, when steamed and pressed, with a beautiful natural polish. When the wheat was reaped with hooks, the stubble was left eight inches or a foot long and so only the finest part of the straw was kept. Later when reaping-machines were used, a coarser plait was introduced, made from the thick straw near the ground.

The straw was drawn by hand, a labourer standing astride three sheaves of wheat and pulling it out in handfuls by the ears. These were cut off and separately threshed, and the clean reed was sold in bundles of eighty pounds. The straws were cut into slips or lengths close by the joints and graded according to fineness, different grades being used for the various patterns of plait. Before use the straws were sometimes dyed and split into threes, fives or sevens by "machines": small hand tools with a sharp point and several radiating blades or fins. Having been steamed and bleached, they were passed through mills or rollers to prevent them from breaking and were then worked into plait.

The commonest sort was made by boys and children and paid for at the rate of fivepence a score (twenty yards). It was quite usual for children to be made to plait a score between coming out of school and going to play. For troublesome and elaborate plaits women were often paid half a crown or three shillings a score and so were able to earn eighteen shillings a week, while their husbands got only sixteen shillings a week as labourers.

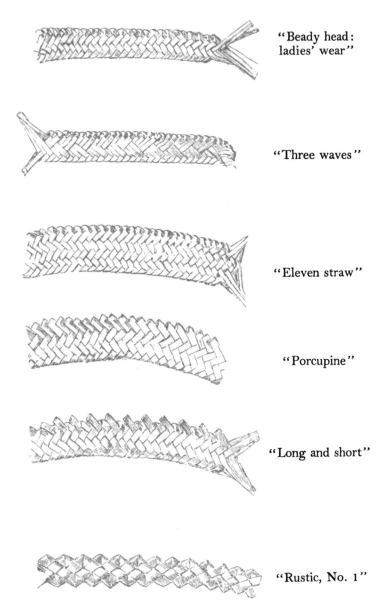

"Beady head:
ladies' wear"

"Three waves"

"Eleven straw"

"Porcupine"

"Long and short"

"Rustic, No. 1"

Hertfordshire straw-plait

They had to buy the straw which they used, but this was not a heavy proportion of the cost. Thirty yards of fine plait or twenty-six of coarser quality went to make a hat. No doubt it is a craft which could well be revived with much advantage to many British farmers and cottagers, but it has been almost killed by Japanese plaits and coarse rye-straw imported from France.

These two letters from the Hertfordshire woman who made the plaits which are here illustrated are so much better than anything else I can say about this graceful rural art that they may be added without apology.

"Sir,

I am sending you the patterns of Plait that you ask for trusting they will be what you want and as you would like them to be but I want you to take in to consideration that it is quite 30 Years since I have done any but the Rustic for after the death of my Parents I went out to Service for some years as Cook and Cookhousekeeper and Workinghousekeeper and when I come home the only sort going was the Rustic but I know how to do it but when one goes from 4 to 11 it does seem as if one cant get along but all that one wants is patients and I am like my Parents I always see my work done in my own mind before I begin and I don't think their is much to complain about but with more practise more perfection my Cousins house where you went to ask if I lived their she is quite taken with the three Wave and now I think that is all I have to say hoping it is not so cold where you are as it is here now as to the cost of my time I dont think if I say 2/- and postage you can think it to much it aint the time it takes to do the Patterns but the time it takes to get ones fingers to a certain form as all are different make of work and the hand has to get a different form of movement.

Yours Faithfully,

E— F—

I am sorry that I did not know that Mr Davis had retired from farming but did not tell you about him to make a stupid of you all I knew was what Mr Jeffs told me and I cant say how long it is ago for time flies so fast one is not always awear of its speed."

The reply to my letter with the money:

"Sir,

I have know doubt by this time you are beginning to think my a very carless sort of a person in keeping you so long with out an answear to your letter I received on Monday morning but when I tell you the cause you will understand and yow know we have had a very sharp spell of cold weather and Gardening was put in the back grounds but when the longed for change came one had to put in all their time and that with a will I have got my Beans, Peas, Carrots, and Parsnips in I was very pleased to hear that the Pattens where all that yow wished them to be and trusting that it may be the right work in the right place thanking you very much for the Order.

Yours Faithfully.

E— F—"

Rough straw or stubble can be made into very good door-mats. It is simply a matter of braiding in three and tucking under every few inches of plait a long handful of straw, which is taken up in the next coil of plait.

Rush-plaiting with sedge, for making workmen's baskets, is a country industry which was revived at Micheldever in Hampshire about thirty years ago, and more recently, for mats and other useful things, in Dorset and elsewhere.

Chapter XI

MAKING SPICKS

IN anticipation of the season's work, the thatcher must be furnished with a stock of thatching spars, which are straight, pointed sticks on which twine is wound to hold on the thatch, or else spicks, which are sticks twisted double with a point at each end, like a hair-pin. April or May, before haymaking begins, is the time for this work, for there is then plenty of lately-cut wood, hazel or sallow, still green enough to be twisted without snapping.

The elder generation of men who did, and still do, this work belong either to the class of thatchers or to those woodmen who make hurdles, faggots and fencing-stakes and are skilled hedgers. My first teacher of this craft was William Jones, of Kingsdown, Wiltshire, whose family have been thatchers for three or four generations. His name for the double points is "spekes", and he is doubtless right in preferring the work done with these to the more slovenly practice, common in Wiltshire, of using spars. These latter are single-pointed sticks a couple of feet long, which are driven into the thatch so that the points lie higher than the heads; the twine is simply turned round them and tightened over the thatch by driving in the spar a little further, so as to press it down.

There are, besides these, two kinds of spick; the single-twist, for general use on ricks, and double-twist, for house-thatching or where neatness of finish matters. There is a difference of opinion among thatchers as to which sort is the more lasting; but before speaking of this, the process of their making had better be described.

The thatcher works in a little hut made of faggots, seated either upon a stool or astride a bench with a short upright bar fixed in one end of it, to assist him in cleaving the wood. He first chooses clean sticks of one to two inches in thickness, trims off all projecting twigs, and cuts them off to a length of about four feet six inches. When he has thus got ready several dozen, he sets to work to split them into fours, fives, or sixes, according to their stoutness, using for this work a small billhook with a blade not more than nine inches long and an inch and a half broad; and with the same tool he points these rods at either end.

The twist is made thus. The split stick is held in the middle by both hands, the thumbs pressed hard under it and close together, the bark side of the wood being upwards, then, both together, the left is brought down vertically and the right turned down and inwards, so that the palm is towards you. The reader, if he should try to do this, will observe that its success depends upon the ends of the thumbs being harder than the fibres of the stick; in thatchers' hands this is the general rule.

In making double-twist spicks a second bend is made in the other direction, so that the bark instead of being twisted over goes straight across from side to side and the under or cleft side of the wood comes inwards all the time. Some say that by this means the wood is better protected and lasts longer, others on the contrary that in the single-twist the fibres are more closely pressed together and so admit the wet less easily. Many labourers twist spicks anyhow, by treading on one end and wrenching the other over, but this is almost certain to tear the wood and so spoil the spick that even if it can be used once, it will be perished before another rick is made.

After a great number of spicks have been twisted, the

thatcher takes a long flexible willow-twig and twirls it
into a ring, barely large enough to span his bundle of a
hundred spicks. Two splinters of wood are stuck cross-
wise in this, one having its point fixed in the earth, so
that the ring stands upright, and the other pointed horizontally towards him. He then kneels on the ground
and counts the spicks, taking them towards him two at a
time, with both hands alternately—two, four, six, eight,
and so on up to five score. When the hundred spicks
have been counted, they are laid with points set just into
the willow circle, from alternate sides; and by the time
there are fifty in the ring, the horizontal splinter has
been pushed well above half-way in the ring. Soon it is

taken out, and it may take
some trouble to get in the
last few spicks; but if their
points are once inserted,
that is enough for the present. Now two bonds or
withs are needed, for the
bundle is to be tied at each
end. A withy rod more than
three feet long is taken, and
its thinner end twisted into
a loop, through which the
stouter end is passed. It is
put round the spicks about
six inches from the end and
drawn as tight as possible,
the thatcher pressing his
foot on the bundle and tug-
ging against it. Now a

Single-twist   Double-twist
    spick   spick

firm and sharp turn is given to the rod where it comes
through the loop, so that the twist holds it down securely

and the long end lies straight down the bundle. A similar
with is tied round the other end, and the long ends of each
with are pushed inside the opposite loops. The bundle
is driven together tightly and neatly by beating its ends
on the ground or giving them a few blows with the flat
of the billhook. Thus each bundle is finished, and stacked
with the rest, like rounds of ammunition, against the end
wall of the hut.

STRAW-BONDS AND HAY-BONDS

TWINERS, THROW-CROOKS, THUMB-BONDS AND WIMBLES

There are many ways of making bonds of straw or hay.
The most usual is by means of a hook called a twister,
twiner or throw-crook. This is generally an iron hook
turning in a wooden handle; but there are different
sorts and the older ones are all of wood. The Anglesey
thatcher fastens two of these into a twisted straw belt,
and he walks backwards turning the handles while two
helpers make the bonds. Each single length of straw-
rope is rolled into a ball, the end of one is spliced to the
end of the other and the two then twisted together on
one hook. In the hands of a skilful man this will save
time, but an ordinary labourer had better twist each
bond singly, for it is difficult to serve two assistants
without confusion, and it is important that the bond
shall be tight and regular. This is by no means the only
way to twist bonds. Some labourers make them simply
on a short stick, the straw being looped over one end,
and the bond made by one man while the other twirls
the stick round and round; one man alone can make them
with hay.

Making straw-bonds is a good wet-day occupation,

and in some barns dozens of them are to be seen laid by
for use; not only long ones for thatching, but shorter
ones for tying trusses of hay, straw or beans.

In several southern counties they make what they call
"thumb-bonds"—"thummle-benes" in Devon—in this
manner. A handful of hay is
pulled partly out of a stack
and twisted tightly till it
forms the beginning of a hay-
bond. This is passed over the
back of the right hand into
the palm, where it is held,
and the hand is moved round
and round so as to twist the
next coil behind the first
one. Thus the bond is at once

A "thummle-bene" (Pons-
worthy, Dartmoor)

twisted and coiled up, the finished part slipping off the
end of the thumb as the bond is formed round the base
of it. To do it well needs practice, but it is easier than
using a wimble single-handed, which is the next, and
last, method of making bonds to be described.

The wimble consists of two wooden bars joined together parallel to one another like the sides of a ladder
by two rungs and having an iron pin passed through
them, upon which the framework can revolve. The pin is
driven horizontally into a post or wall, and a handful of
straw is looped over one end of the nearer bar. The
thatcher then sets the wimble spinning, thus twisting up
the handful of straw into a rope, and as he does so he
adds more straw with his left hand; and thus he continues, turning the wimble by a constant slight movement of the right hand, adding more and more straw to
the rope, and walking backwards as it lengthens. Look
at him, and it seems the easiest and most natural thing

in the world; try it yourself and you will find that this tool obeys none but its master. Part of the secret is to keep the ends of the straw open in each hand, that they may mingle into one another and not push each other out of the way; but the real trouble is to get used to doing a different thing with either hand. The wimble must be kept turning steadily and sufficiently fast or the bond will be slack-twisted and lumpy. This wimble is not often seen, but it is used by a thatcher near Crediton and by his three sons, who are thatchers also and work over an area of twenty miles radius.

There are one or two other local sorts of wimble or spinner, but their use is becoming rare. In Cornwall a rather elaborate pattern, called a "wink"—with crossed ends, having a notch cut out of the tip of each of those in front—was used, but has now almost disappeared, for "coir", or cocoanut fibre rope, is imported into that county and has replaced the native straw-rope in thatching.

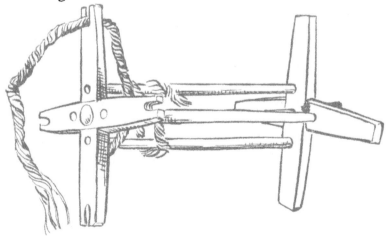

A "wink" (St Pinnock, Liskeard, Cornwall)

YELMING, COMBING AND DRAWING REED

Before straw is fit to be used for thatching it must first be well cleaned; that is, the rough and broken pieces must be taken out so that the stems lie straight and close together, free from all weeds and rubbish, in bundles ready for use. The better this is done, the closer the thatch can be made and the longer will it resist the weather. One of the chief hindrances to thatching now-adays is that the threshing-machine breaks up the straw much more than the flail or the other old methods of threshing did, and so makes it much less durable.

In the simplest method of thus preparing the straw for use, the thatcher or his assistant, kneeling down over an opened bundle of straw, straightens it out handful by handful by drawing it through both hands from the middle; the broken straws thus dragged out he throws aside as unfit for use. This simple process is known in the Midlands as "yelming" or "gabbling" and the bundles of clean straw are sometimes called "yelms". A Sussex thatcher sometimes uses for this job a bean stick which he calls a "duck", thinking it better than using the hands simply. Others in Sussex and Hampshire wet the straw and draw it out by the ends from under a hurdle.

This brings us to the more thorough methods of preparation, called "reed-drawing", which however have been superseded in some districts by a machine patented by Isaacs sixty or seventy years ago and made by various local mechanics; and this I will first briefly describe. It may be fixed on the top of an ordinary steam-driven machine and is hired out to farmers by the proprietors of these engines, who generally travel round with them. The straw is passed over two revolving conical drums, with hooked tines, which catch and carry away all the bent and broken pieces, while the straight unbroken reed is delivered at the tail of the machine by an endless ladder formed of two belts with wooden slats across, which moves over a sloping boarded platform. The broken straw is carried out at the other end of the machine. This method does not do the work so well as drawing by hand, and it is impossible to avoid the damage done by the threshing machine.

Near Taunton the sheaves are still drawn by hand over a comb—sometimes fixed on a trestle, sometimes at the end of a sloping stool, on which the labourer rests one foot. The ears are finished with a hand-comb. Another old method which was practised in North Devon is described by Mr Passmore of Reading University. This was to lay about two dozen wheat-sheaves along the threshing-floor and with a flail to beat the ears; then to take the sheaves two at a time, bring their heads together and, hanging them up by a rope, to comb them through with a hand-comb about a foot wide, with long tines set an inch or more apart; first from heads to butts, then from butts to heads. A certain number of these combed sheaves was called a "nitch". In Southern Ireland reed for thatching is made simply by beating out the grain against a barrel or trestle, taking handfuls of wheat-straw at a time; and this was also done in some parts of Western England.

The traditional way of reed-drawing in Dorset is a more painstaking one. Some twenty or thirty sheaves of unthreshed wheat are placed under a long beam, whose ends are lowered by pegs on two wooden standards about twelve feet apart; the base of this press is a fairly broad bench which stands about two feet from the ground. The ears of wheat project into the barn and the butts are often pressed close against the barn wall. Before the "drawing" begins, the sheaves are trodden down and the beam is adjusted to hold them tightly, though not immovably. The labourers then stand before the press and draw out the wheat swiftly by handfuls with the right hand, supporting them in the left hand so that the straw may not be broken. Thus the flag or leaf is stripped from the stem, and any weeds and rubbish which may be in the sheaf are left behind in the press. The ears are then cut off, either with a sickle or else against a scythe-blade fixed so as to project from the wall of the barn, and they must be collected for threshing later. The clean reed is weighed into bundles of fourteen pounds, which are tied and stumped on the ground once or twice, to level the butts. This is without any doubt the best way of preparing straw for thatching; but the strength of the straw depends on the soil which grows it. The best kind of wheat for the purpose is standard red, which in the neighbourhood of Bridport (where, on a few farms, reed-drawing is still practised) will produce fourteen or fifteen sacks of grain per acre; but because of its greater yield (sixteen or eighteen sacks on the same ground) white victor is generally used.

In Somerset and Dorset wheat-straw goes by the name of reed; and reed-thatched ricks are to be seen on many farms between Wyke Regis, Bridport and Ilminster, and are at once recognisable from their shape and the way in which each handful can be seen distinctly, held down by its own spick. Most of this reed is consumed where it is produced, but there is a fairly keen demand for the remainder, for finishing house-thatches. For this purpose it is nearly ideal; it is short enough to be easily handled, it lies all one way and, being free from ears and flags does not hold the wet, for the rain shoots easily off it. Five or six years ago it was thought worth while to thatch a row of cottages between Newbury and Hungerford with Dorset reed; and on some cottages it is known to have stood for over forty years without need of renovation.

Reed-drawing is an occupation for wet days in the winter and was formerly paid at the rate of a penny a bundle, forty bundles being thought a fair day's work for two women and a man. Readers of Thomas Hardy will remember that it was one of Tess's labours at Flintcomb-Ash Farm. In those days farmers would supply the labourers with cider, and they, if they had finished the agreed number by four o'clock, would sometimes be ashamed to leave so early and go on working till five. At present the cost of production is five times as great, and the market value of the reed has by no means increased proportionately; the farmer may think himself lucky if he gets many more than a dozen bundles drawn from his press in the day, for he will hardly get it undertaken as piece-work.

THATCHING

Any account of haymaking and harvesting would be very incomplete without a description of the process of thatching. Rick-thatching and house-thatching are two very different jobs, and though in principle there is often some relation between them, in each particular district there are, besides local fashions, endless differences in the practice of individual thatchers, which it would take too long to do more than indicate. I shall therefore describe the common manner of rick-thatching near Bath, with which I happen to be most familiar, and then try to give an idea of some of the varieties of thatching in other places. If this should meet the eye of any expert in the craft I hope it will be read with indulgence; for it is very far from being my intention to teach him his business.

The rick is left by the haymakers as nearly as possible in its final shape. The sides have been carefully squared and any loose hay raked off, the top is built up into a ridge and the sides symmetrically sloped. But it is not in the nature of hay to be put into a very clean and sharp form, and by the time the thatcher comes to it the stack has been left to settle down for a week or two and has lost several feet of height; it may also have been damaged by winds, so a little more raking may be needed, the rakings being put back on the top of the stack, and if the stack has a ridge or a point which is not sharp enough, it may be made up to the required height with a few bundles of oat-straw.

The thatcher is provided with a ladder and an iron hook to hold it to the ground when he is working round a corner, a pair of shears, a spear or spike to support his bundle of thatch, a couple of broad leather pads to kneel upon, a rope with a ring spliced into one end to carry up his straw, and a thatching-rake, which is a cudgel four or five feet long with a dozen long iron teeth in one end of it, driven through at intervals of a couple of inches. He also needs to have a tub of water close at hand, enough wheat- or rye-straw for the thatch, and one or two bundles of spicks or thatching-spars.

He dips each bundle of straw into the water, first at one end, then at the other, so that it is all well wetted. Then kneeling over it, he unties it and draws the straw in handfuls through both hands from the middle of the bundle, thus separating any broken or bent straws and getting it to lie all one way. This is the ordinary way of yelming; and an armful of the straw thus prepared, locally called "yelms", is taken up the ladder in the rope and secured against the spear, which is driven into the hay wherever it may be most conveniently to hand.

The thatch is commenced along the eaves, by laying handfuls of straw side by side to form a horizontal "lane" or "strake", with ears upwards and butts downwards, projecting slightly lower than the eaves are intended finally to remain. The handfuls of yelms are spread out flat, so as to lie not more than two or three inches deep, and are fixed about a foot from their lower ends by pegging across them a twist of straw which forms the beginning of a bond. The thatcher works round the rick from right to left, shifting his ladder along as he goes, without needing to descend except for fresh supplies of thatch. As each fresh handful of yelms is laid the last one is tapped and raked with the thatching rake till it lies evenly, the free end of the bond being temporarily pegged back so as not to be in the way of the next section of work. When this is ready, enough fresh straw is added to the end of the bond to leave some overlapping, and it is twisted and pegged down as before. The spicks are driven in by a blow of the hand, which is generally protected by a stout piece of leather in the form of the palm of a glove, though sometimes a small wooden mallet is used. It is very important that the spicks be driven in with their points directed rather upwards, or the rain will run down them and rot the hay. Each handful or "feed" of thatch must overlap that on its right, as well as those immediately below it.

A section of three or four lanes is laid at the same time to save going repeatedly round the rick, and on a small rick the thatcher may work to the very top; but the lower lanes must always be kept longer than the next above them. Each lane overlaps the one below it by about half the length of the straw, and the bond which fixes it comes midway across the overlapping. The second lane and all those above it are laid with butts upwards and ears downwards, until the ridge is reached. The corners of the rick are rounded and thus the number of handfuls in each lane is gradually diminished.

When the ridge is reached, the two rows of straw-butts which come together from either side are shaken and worked into each other so as to interlock. Some thatchers bend over the last few inches and spring them into one another, so as to make a still neater and tighter finish, but this is not often thought necessary. When all is finished, the thatcher trims the eaves with a small pair of shears, such as are used for sheep-shearing, and rakes up the ends of straw and other rubbish before he goes.

It is quite common to fasten a thatch of this sort somewhat differently, holding down each lane with a bond near the upper part of it, which is overlapped by the next one. In this way only two bonds show in the finished thatch, one just below the ridge and another one, which is added to secure the lower ends of the bottom "lane", just above the eaves.

RICK-THATCHING: NORFOLK

In Norfolk the ricks are thatched, as in most other places, with ordinary wheat-straw, but the traditional way of thatching haystacks in this county has nearly disappeared owing to the use of twine instead of straw-bonds, and as it is rather ingenious it may be thought worthy of a brief account.

Straw-bonds, made with a twister, and straight pegs or broaches of split nut-wood are used to fix the thatch, but only one bond is used along the eaves, to hold the lowest strake of thatch, and three or four near the ridge. The intermediate strakes, three or four in number, are tucked under the hay at their uppermost ends and these are then overlapped by the butts of the next strake. The ends of the rick are upright, and these intermediate strakes on either side are held by straw-bonds twisted alternately over and under two rows of broaches, in the form of a zigzag, at either end of the rick. As the hay is cut, the bonds are set back into another zigzag to hold the edges of the thatch; and this is found in practice to secure it perfectly.

In Norfolk and Cambridgeshire a round-roofed rick is called a cob, while a long rick of hay or wheat is called a jug.

WEXING

Sometimes the side of a shed or a very steeply sloped roof of a barn or skillen is covered with thatch; or a haystack may have subsided, exposing one of its sides to damage by rain, so that this must be thatched to protect it. This work is called wexing, and it is more difficult than ordinary thatching, because the straw will not lie on the slope before it is fastened, but needs to be held up by one man while the other fixes it; and so two men are needed to wex the side of a rick and three to do the side or roof of a building. Some Kentish farmers thatched their long wheat-ricks right to the ground; the upright part was put on last and called the "petticoat".

THATCHING-MATERIALS AND HOUSE-THATCHING

A good many materials can be used for thatching, and that is usually chosen which is most easily obtained in each district; in Norfolk river-reed, in Essex rushes, in Dorset reed made from wheat-straw, in parts of Somerset rye-straw, which is grown solely for this purpose and cut while green; in most other places wheat- or oat-straw from the threshing-machine, on moors and mountains furze, heather or bracken. Heather is capable of making a very good and enduring thatch. At Rougham in Suffolk some cottages have been very successfully thatched with the stems of flax which has been grown for linseed and cut with the reaping-machine; in this state it is too old and coarse for making into linen, and it is also unsuitable for bedding cattle as it will not decompose into farmyard manure. There are many local materials; for example in Shropshire, near Bishop's Castle, meadowrush mixed with dock and other weeds is used on haystacks; between Wimborne and Poole a kind of spear-grass which grows in the salt marshes; while near Petworth, where wooden barrel-hoops are made, the shavings from them have been used for thatching sheds and cottages, though perhaps never on ricks. In Southern Ireland, as in parts of Scotland, it was the practice of thatchers to tie strips of turf to the rafters or lintels along the eaves; these provided a hold for the points of the "scollops", or spars, and were called the "fill-beam".

The best and most lasting material for house-thatching is river-reed, which is used by the Norfolk thatchers and in Holland and has been known to last, with little or no repair, for well over a century.

Reed is also the name given in Somerset and Dorset to clean, straight wheat-straw, with the ears cut off and the flags stripped. This is generally used for the outer coat only of a house-thatch, being laid on about nine inches deep pegged with spicks on to the inner coat, or "waistcoat", of ordinary straw thatch, which is sewn on to the rafters first to a thickness of at least a foot.

Before use the bundles of straw are placed on end and

thoroughly wetted, three buckets of water to each bundle. In Dorset the thatcher uses a wooden tool called a "bowl" to carry the bundles on to the roof; it is somewhat like a hod intended for straw instead of bricks. Two men are required, one inside and one outside the rafters, to sew it on, using tar-rope in a steel needle a foot long. The man below gives a tap to show where his hand is, and the man above puts through the needle cautiously, lest he should spike the other. Thus the tar-rope is twisted round and round the horizontal rafters or battens and tied sometimes to the intersection of these and the slanting rafters. Each strake (or lane) of straw when laid is raked down with the thatching-comb, the butts driven up into the right positions with the "biddle" or drift, and brought level with the paring-knife.

The final coat of reed is laid very carefully, especially round the corners, or over dormers, where it must be given something of a twist so that the rain may shoot off the ends of the straw and not settle into the hollows. Where the dormers project steeply, or in other sharp corners, a piece of lead may be sewn in as a gutter for the water to run down. This coat is fixed with spars driven in to the "waistcoat", inclined upwards a little, so as not to make holes for the rain to get in. Along the top and bottom pieces of split wood called ledgers and slats are fixed to hold it. These slats are laid in a diamond formation, called "dimenting", crossing each other alternately above and below, and are then pegged down with spars over their crossings, the pegs in the middle going horizontally and those above and below set vertically[1].

[1] For this description I am indebted to Mr Young, thatcher, of Briantspuddle, Dorset; and for the following one of a thatch composed entirely of reed, to Mr Thomas, thatcher, of Salway Ash, near Bridport.

Where reed is used throughout in making a new thatch, a different method is employed. A thin layer of reed, called the lining-reed, is first sewn to the rafters scarcely more than two or three motes thick, the ends of these only just overlapped by those above them. At the ridge and overs (or eaves) this is reinforced by wads of reed, those at the overs being laid upwards, following the slope of the roof and overhanging by about nine inches, and being closely tied above, they take the form of wedges. Over these the coat is laid, in sittings (strakes or lanes) as with a rick, and again sewn on; the first sitting covering the lower wads completely and being fixed all the way along by a rod called a "tying ledger"; the next sitting overlapping the first by six or eight inches, the third and fourth likewise. The ridge is strengthened by wads laid lengthwise horizontally, one row at either side and one along the summit; and over these more sittings of reed are laid and fixed with spars (spicks) and two ledgers, generally with a "diamonding" of short sticks crossing between the ledgers.

A thatch of this sort is reckoned to last for forty years and often lasts much longer with but little repair, and though reed is shorter than ordinary wheat-straw it makes a cleaner and neater job and can be more nicely adjusted and shaped. The thatcher's chief tools here consist of a bowl for carrying up the reed, and a biddle or drift, a wooden tool with rounded ridges running lengthwise on its face and cut across by transverse grooves, for knocking up the butts. If an old thatch is being patched or renewed, he will also have a spear for holding the reed to the roof and a short hook or paring-knife for cutting away the old rotten thatch. In this work, where the thatch is not entirely stripped, the rafters and laths must first be made good where necessary, and the holes

where the thatch is quite perished must be filled up with
long bundles of ordinary straw thatch, tied on, till the
surface is made up to one level. Then the reed is pegged
on with short spars, which are sometimes joined by
horizontal ledgers.

Haystacks are thatched with reed in a very simple and
effective manner. The handfuls are laid somewhat aslant
and slightly overlapping one another, beginning in sittings or rows along the eaves and working upwards, so
that when finished there is a certain twist in their direction from the ridge outwards and downwards. Each
bundle is fixed on with a spick, of which one end is set
obliquely and the other directly into the hay, the latter
passing through the overlapped portion of the bundle
next beside it. Along the ridge the handfuls of reed are
set into each other and cocked out somewhat at either
end of it. The spars may be fixed either in the middle of
each handful, so that they all show, or near the end, so
that only the first and last row can be seen. These ricks
are rectangular and inclined to be square.

REED-THATCHING: NORFOLK AND CAMBRIDGESHIRE

Thatching with river-reed is at present in considerable
demand, and much has been done lately by the Norfolk
thatchers in many parts of the British Isles. River-reed
is much less inflammable than straw; there is hardly any
risk from sparks, for there are several smithies in Norfolk
whose roofs have been thatched with reed for a century
or more, and to make it yet more safe the reed can be
dipped in a fire-proofing solution before it is applied.

Reed is cut on the broads between Christmas and
April, when it has become quite dry and hard, almost

like cane, and the leaves have fallen to the ground; the flower is not cut off. The reed-cutters tie it in bundles of such a size that six of them laid together, with three butt-ends each way, measure a fathom, or six feet, in circumference. This is locally called a "fallom" of reed.

In some old reed-thatches in Norfolk and Cambridgeshire split and peeled brambles were used to tie the bundles on to the rafters, and other bundles were woven through these to form the foundation of the thatch, but for many years it has been the practice of house-thatchers, here as elsewhere, to have the rafters crossed with battens and to sew the bundles of reed on to these with tar-rope. The bundles of reed are put on whole, and "faced up" by tapping them with the leggatt, or drift, which is a somewhat large tool here, having instead of wooden ridges several rows of old horse-nails beaten flat, whose sides act as little hammers to drive the butts of the reeds up to the required positions. The reed is sewn on to the battens twelve inches thick. At the ridge it is cut off vertically, since it is too stiff to be satisfactorily bent over, and a cap or shell is made of sedge, to cover it and keep the wet out of the joint. This shell is perhaps six inches thick and the material is of the nature of rough, sharp blades or grasses. It is held down by a network or diamonding of split hazel, fixed by double broaches, or "single-twist spicks" as they are called elsewhere. The fashion of "herring-boning" in place of "diamonding", of making other fancy patterns of split hazel "runners" and of working the edges of the outer layers of reed into ornamental shapes has been introduced in the last forty or fifty years by the family of Mr Farman of Salhouse near Wroxham, who is one of the best-known practitioners of the craft.

Chapter XII

THRESHING

"Why, here were vourteen men, some years agoo,
A-kept a-drashen half the winter drough;
An' now woone's drashels be'n't a bit of good.
They got machines to drashy in', plague teäke 'em!
An' he that vust vound out the way to meäke 'em,
I'd drash his busy-zides vor'n if I could!
Avore they took away our work, they ought
To meäke us up the bread our leäbour bought."

W. BARNES.

GRAIN may be threshed, trodden or combed out of the ear; it may also be crushed out with sledges. The last method seems to be confined to the East, but the first three have till lately been practised in this country. The typical threshing implement in England, however, till towards the close of last century was the flail, and it may therefore claim the first place in description.

The flail consists of two chief parts, the hand-staff, a straight and slender ash-stick some four or five feet long, and the swingel, fringel, or beater, a shorter and stouter cudgel of holly, blackthorn or some other tough heavy wood. The hand-staff might last a lifetime, but a couple of winters' hard use was enough to wear out the swingel; and in the autumn men would look about in the hedges for a likely bit of knotty crab-stick to serve for the following season. In the West of England, where the complete tool was known as a drashel, the beater alone was called the "vliel". The proportion of these two parts is by no means constant, a longer and heavier swingel being needed for threshing oats than for wheat or barley.

The most effective form of joint between these two parts is the cap or runner, made in the form of a swivel from a slip of ash or occasionally from ram's-horn, steamed and bent over a knob or nail at the extremity of the hand-staff and bound on so as to revolve upon it. This forms a loop to which the swingel is fastened by a leather thong or else with a "whang" of eelskin. The end of the swingel is often drilled with several holes, and a leather thong sewn through, to which the other thong joining the runner is linked.

Flail-joint (Norfolk)

This, however, is by no means the only way of joining the two parts. In Ireland a groove is cut round one end of each stick, and the two are linked together with a gad of twisted withy-wood or a double loop of plaited leather. In North Wales they may be similarly joined with a thong of raw hide; though a short chain is often used, which turns on a swivel made by the blacksmith or is simply fixed to the head of the hand-staff and passed through a hole in the beater, so that every time it is swung round it must recover itself by twirling the opposite way in mid-air.

In using the flail, the hand-staff is grasped with both hands a little apart and raised and sharply swung so that the swingel flies round the labourer's head and comes down with a clipping blow on the ears of corn before him. If the right hand is nearest to the end of the hand-staff, the right foot is placed forward and the flail swung

from left to right. The swingel must pass well over the
head, above all where two men thresh together, for then
they strike in turn and must keep their flails out of each
other's way.

Oats, barley and beans are often threshed loose, and
in such cases the two men work across the threshing-
floor in a zigzag, passing one another in the middle.
Wheat is threshed in sheaves, about a dozen being un-
tied and arranged in two rows, with the ears together
and butts outwards; the threshers stand at either end,
working briskly and in time with one another. After
about half a minute, they change the position of their
hands, put the other foot forward, and swing their flails
the other way. A skilful thresher hardly ever touches
the sheaves with his hands; he can turn them over by a
quick movement of the flail or, grasping the two parts
of it together, push the straw into a heap as though with
a pike. The last of the grain is taken out by knocking the
sheaf against a stone or barrel.

Most of the old barns throughout the country were
built for flail-threshing and made in three divisions.
There was a strip in the middle with the barn-door at
one end, high enough to drive a loaded waggon through;
this was the threshing-floor, and it was cut off from the
spaces on either side, which were known as the barn's
mows, by low boarded partitions called the mowsteads.
The sheaves of corn were loaded into the mow on one
side and threshed bit by bit in the middle, the empty
straw being stacked in the opposite mow. The threshing-
floor was sometimes made merely of hard beaten earth,
chalk and clay, or clay and cow-dung; occasionally it was
of stone, but in the best barns oak or elm planks were
used, tongued together with strips of iron, so that the
grain should not fall through. Lombardy poplar was a

wood which was recommended for this purpose, as being proof against the gnawing of rats and mice. The barndoor was made in two parts which opened outwards and ended two or three feet short of the ground. The lower portion could be closed with a partition called the rack, which slid into grooves at either side, so that the doors could be opened to admit light and air without making the threshing-floor immediately accessible to the whole farmyard population. Another part of the barn which must be mentioned is the cove or cupboard, a boarded division by the end of the threshing-floor, where the grain could be kept before it was winnowed and taken to the granary.

Many of the larger barns have two threshing-floors and sometimes a door at either end, so that the waggon could be driven right through; though more often the only other doors are small ones made simply for the convenience of the men. It is rare now to see a barn used in this way, for flail-threshing has become extinct in nearly all those districts in which the finest barns exist; and the fact that they are needlessly large for most other purposes and not as a rule very handy for storing large machinery is a great reason why so many of these splendid buildings have been pulled down or allowed to decay.

The business of threshing used to last all the winter, and on large farms certain labourers devoted all their time to it. These specialists could easily be distinguished from the outdoor work-folk by the whiteness of their complexions; yet they were often, it is said, much annoyed if their master sent them off to do unaccustomed jobs: to spread muck, for example, or to serve the cattle. Flail-threshing was hard, monotonous and dusty work, with attendant abuses and annoyances both to master

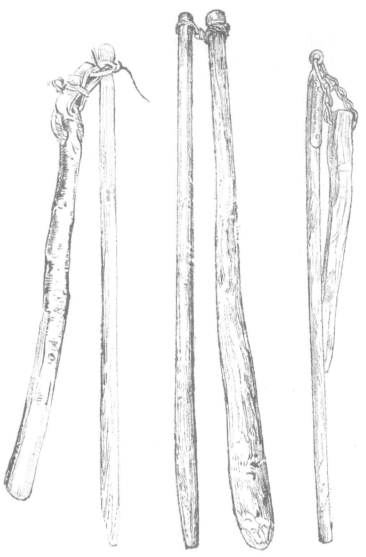

Cornish (Mousehole) Irish (in use at Rath- Welsh (in use in
          coursey, Co. Cork, in the Elan Valley
              1930)   in 1930)

Flails

and men. Many of the old writers refer to the farmer's losses from "foul threshing"—that is, when some of the grain was still left in the straw—and from "pilfering". The latter crime, one would think, might almost be forgiven, when wages, till well within living memory, were in some places only seven or eight shillings a week; and though a man might increase his earnings to as much as nine or ten shillings by working early and late by candlelight, farmers were sometimes so mean as to reduce the money for piece-work when so much more had been done; and against this extortion there was no redress. Such complaints as this, it must be said, were nearly always made, not against well-to-do landowners, but against small farmers with little capital, who have from their circumstances generally been the hardest employers.

There is an old saying in Essex that the sound of threshing would tell one how the work was being paid; a slow, dull thumping announcing "by the day, by the day", while piece-work would induce a brisker rhythm: "we-took-it, we-took-it, we-took-it!"—a maddening sort of joke, one would think, to be dinned for hours on end into the ears of any labourer, so busied, who should bear it in mind.

At the present time there are very few districts in England where flail-threshing is regularly practised. It is principally used in parts of Essex, Suffolk and Cambridgeshire for beans intended for sowing, since they are thus liable to less damage than from the threshing-machine; though the latter, if worked slowly and without some of its beaters, can be made to answer nearly as well. After the bean-harvest half a dozen men often work together, sometimes threshing out-of-doors on a long cloth and keeping time like a company of bell-ringers; and with peas and beans it is well to thresh in the open on account of the clouds of black dust which are knocked out of them. Clover and grasses are also occasionally threshed by the flail; and a certain Gloucestershire farmer always used it for threshing sainfoin or "French seed", as he called it. A few small-holders, or farmers in mountainous places where it is worth nobody's while to haul round a threshing-machine, still use the flail for all their threshing.

To return to the other methods of threshing which were first mentioned: it was not uncommon forty or fifty years ago in Somersetshire and Gloucestershire for wheat to be "whipped out", that is knocked out by taking it in handfuls and beating the ears against a stone, a trestle, or a barrel with a chain fastened across its end; this was done especially when the straw was wanted unbroken for thatching. It is still a common thing in South-Western Ireland, where in many cottages a room is cleared for the purpose after harvest; they call it "threshing in the kitchen". In the same country oats are half-threshed in this way or with flails, the heavier grain being taken out and the lighter given with the straw to the cattle, a practice seemingly wasteful, but in truth sound economy on farms which cannot grow enough turnips or mangels.

Corn was now and then trodden out by driving bullocks through the threshing-floor, in Norfolk at any rate, and I believe in Kent. An old farmer in the latter county remembers an old white mare which was used for this work every year. "She would put her front feet together and slide down the straw into the barn, as clever as a boy!"

Combs, such as are used for combing reed near Taunton, were also sometimes used for separating the grain from the ears; and a patent on this principle was

taken out by the Rev. Wm. Winlaw in 1795, but it
seems to be a process which was never widely used.
Winlaw's machine was in fact nothing more than a frame
of two crossed bars with an upright comb at each corner,
through which the ears were drawn by hand. But there
were already several forms of rotary threshing-machine,
some worked by horses and other small ones which two
men turned with a crank. One of these (made by John
Winter, of Bawtry, Yorkshire) consisted of a frame
with a revolving horizontal bar, to which short flails
were attached. (An almost exactly similar machine,
called a zakkenklopper, is used for knocking the meal
out of flour-bags in a Dutch windmill.) Another machine
was in the form of a mangle, with short pegs in the upper
drum, which fitted loosely into holes in the lower one,
as the handle was turned. Yet another form had four
boards, set at right angles to one another, turning on a
spindle and having a row of spikes at their outer edges
which passed between the bars of a grating.

It is not within the scope of this book to follow the
history of the development of the threshing-machine in
detail nor to recall the rural disturbances of 1820, which
led to so many extremely severe sentences on labourers
who were concerned in smashing and burning these
labour-saving inventions. It is enough to say that the
two last-mentioned types of thresher may be taken as
the prototypes of the two which have survived till the
present.

One of these is the so-called Scotch thresher, in which
the grain is separated by passing between a barred
grating and a drum studded with short blunt spikes. The
other has a number of arms rotating on a spindle, and to
the outer edge of each arm is fixed a flat wrought-iron
bar with oblique grooves across it; the ears pass between

these and a concave surface and thus the grain is knocked
out of them. The former principle was used on a small
threshing-machine worked by hand, which may be still
in use in very remote places. It is an upright machine,
with a seat in front for one man, who puts the sheaves
into a hopper before him and by working two foot-
treadles assists the action of the machine, the main power
being provided by one or two men who turn the drum
by means of a crank at the side. I have seen this machine
used in Ireland, but it was such very severe labour that
it seemed unbelievable that men could work it for six or
eight hours together, as they are said to have done.

Threshing-machines of the "drum-and-beaters" type
were used on most of the smaller farms throughout the
country and were driven by a horse-gear, which could,
as a rule, be used also for working a chaff-cutting or
root-slicing machine. But these have gradually given
place to internal-combustion engines, though they survive in parts of Scotland and Wales. The horse-works
consisted of a long beam, or crossed beams, to which
one, two or four horses could be harnessed, and the
power was communicated from a crown wheel in the
middle by a horizontal shaft, with an intermediate gear
to the barn-machinery. A round house was often built
against the side of the barn to shelter this horse-works,
especially if it were one of massive wooden construction,
erected by a country millwright. Some of these had a
seat in the middle for the driver, but many were cheap
cast-iron affairs put up in a corner of the yard and a man
had to lead the horses round all the time. Save that it
was fixed, and had a cobbled path made for the horse and
man, it was very much like the horse-works which are
only just being replaced by oil-engines for working the
elevators in the hayfields. Some years ago hundreds of

these old horse-gears were dismantled and broken up by dealers in scrap-iron, when that commodity fetched a better price than it does to-day.

Here and there one meets with a fairly old type of threshing-machine, which has been going for sixty or seventy years; and it may be observed in passing that there is a tendency for steam-engines to be employed less as the motive force and internal combustion engines to take their place; nor are there now nearly so many steam traction-engines on the road as in former years. The modern improved threshing-machine delivers the corn winnowed and cleaned of other seeds, but with the old types the chaff had to be separated after threshing by winnowing.

WINNOWING

The simplest and no doubt, in this country, the most primitive way of separating the corn from the chaff with which it was mixed after threshing was to wait for a windy day, and then standing on a stool to shake it through a sieve over a cloth or a boat's sail, into which the heavy grain fell, while the lighter parts were blown away. This method of winnowing was practised by small-holders in the West of England, when they used to thresh with flails, and is still to be seen in outlying parts of Scotland and Ireland.

A fairly old-established form of winnowing machine, which is now quite given up, was used in barns throughout the country. It was a wooden contrivance, with arms somewhat like those of a reaper-and-binder, but heavier, to which sacks were nailed, so that when they were rotated by a handle a strong draught was created. Sir Walter Scott records that when this machine was brought into Scotland from the Netherlands, during the eighteenth century, a certain minister preached a flaming sermon against the farmer who had dared to thwart Providence by producing a wind "for his ain particular use, instead of waiting till it should please the Lord to send one!" While one man worked this machine another would throw the grain and chaff across the current of air with a barn-shovel, so that the grain fell short and the chaff was blown beyond. The lighter grains fell on the far side of the heap and were called "tailings". It was usual to get rid of the worst part of the chaff first by passing the threshed wheat through a screen or riddle; that is, a wide round sieve with a mesh of rushes or split willow. In Kent a sort of tray, called a shaw, was sometimes used, which combined the uses of the sieve and shovel. It was made of a single broad piece of beech or sycamore, hollowed out like a butcher's tray, and held in both hands; on this the corn and chaff were first shaken, so as to bring the chaff to the top and get rid of some of it, and then thrown across the draught of the winnower.

Another old device for taking small seeds out of grain may be mentioned; this was also used in Kent by millers and was known as a scry. It was like a pair of steps with a wire screen on one side of it, and hung from a hole in the store-room at an angle of forty-five degrees. The corn was shot down it and over the wires; and two or three slanting cross-pieces, called baffle-plates, prevented it from bouncing away, while all the dust and smaller seeds fell through.

The winnowing machine or blower is quite often to be seen on old-fashioned farms, though it is of course part of the steam- or tractor-driven threshing-machine; and some very self-respecting farmers keep a smutter similar to those in flour mills for cleaning their grain before sending it to market, for they declare that nothing betrays the slovenly farmer more than an ill-cleaned sample of wheat.

The clover-huller is another machine, once distinct and separate, whose work is now included in that of the improved threshing-machine: it need not be particularised here. There is in Saffron Walden Museum an early contrivance for doing this work, consisting simply of a thin iron plate pierced with nail-holes, somewhat like a nutmeg grater. There is also another hand-tool which the engine has rendered useless: that is the barley-hummeller. This was a short stick or handle with a set of vertical blades, parallel to one another and an inch or so apart. It had to be dropped repeatedly on barley, after it was threshed, to cut off the awns, ails, or pill, as the beard of barley is variously called. This is injurious both to pigs and poultry; and in Ireland barley was chopped with a shovel for the same reason. The horse-driven machines did not remove the difficulty, but nowadays it exists no longer.

Chapter XIII

CIDER-MAKING

IT seems that cider is more generally drunk now than it has been in recent years, for its manufacture has been revived in some districts which had come to rely mainly upon beer. The poorness of quality and the increased price of the latter beverage must account for this; for in these needy days a farmer may still be expected to offer bottled beer to cattle-buyers and other callers of some social pretensions, but it is not reasonably to be looked for by his harvest-hands, and cider may well be found more satisfying for his personal and domestic use. In the traditional cider-lands, namely Hereford, Worcester, Monmouth, South Devon, Dorset and Somerset, the process of cider-making has, in the hands of large firms of manufacturers, been changed and modified by mechanical and chemical inventions, so that, while essentially simple in principle, it is hardly in a single detail the same as when, half-a-century ago, it was mainly the concern of country-innkeepers, yeomen farmers, and other rural householders. Nor is the drink itself unchanged in quality and flavour; the gassy, india-rubber-tasting and nearly colourless article of present commerce was formerly unknown, while on the other hand many of the old-fashioned recipes have lapsed. To natives of places where it is made cider is distinguished in the three degrees of "sweet, mild and rough", while that which has got harsh and sour by too long keeping is called "ropy". The standard of taste in cider has probably changed in many generations, as it has certainly differed in several parts of the country. John Phillips, the author of "Cyder: a Poem" (1706)—an incomparable account of the ancient craft of cider-making—tells of connoisseurs of his time who produced subtle varieties of the drink, counterfeiting the flavours of foreign wines. But the old school of cider-fanciers has passed and with it many of the old-established kinds of apple celebrated by Phillips and other writers: thrifts, moiles, musks and pippins; russets, red-streaks, rathe-ripes, bitter-sweets, stubbards, John-apples, cats'-heads and codlins; these have given place to newer types, whose names are sometimes more suggestive of standardised insipidity than of individual character.

Cider-making begins generally in October or November—sometimes later, for the apples are left to mellow, or even partially to rot, before being used. In Hereford and Somerset they are piled in pyramidal heaps in the orchards and so remain for some weeks till the frost has been on them. Then, when all is ready and the year's accumulations of dirt and rubbish cleared from the machinery in the cider-house, they are brought in and ground to pomace; first with "breakers", or toothed iron rollers, geared against one another like those of a mangle, and afterwards more thoroughly with smooth stone rollers. The juice and pulp are collected in a cistern capable of holding some hundreds of gallons; from this some of the liquid is drawn off and the residue is scooped out to be squeezed dry in the press. The ancient form of mill, however, was an immense round stone trough, sometimes ten feet across, in which a ponderous mill-stone, mounted on a horse-drawn axle, revolved upon its edge and crushed the apples in its path. These mills have been generally disused for many years, but they are sometimes to be seen doing duty as feeding-troughs in old farmyards. Mr Moses Barnicoat, of Tregony in Cornwall, thus described a still more primitive local method: "We don't make but a very little cider here, but when we have plenty of apples we throw them in an iron boiler and scrat 'em with the butt-end of a stub. Then we lay the pummy on a thin layer of reed, or oaten straw, at the bottom of the press; turn the ends of straw in, and spread another layer on top; and so we keep piling up, like cheese, till the 'mock' is finished." Then the press is wrung down, and the thick brown juice runs out into a tub, from which the village boys who crowd round to watch, try to suck it up through bits of straw—"fair pigs they be!" But after a few days they get tired of it and enough is left to rack off into a hogshead, where it ferments; and as it overflows, the cask is daily replenished from a jug. After about a fortnight the fermentation is complete, and the new cider is decanted through a strainer into another barrel, an old sherry- or brandy-cask for choice; in a few weeks' time it is in perfect condition.

The old method of squeezing the juice through straw is peculiar to the south-western counties and is there continued by many farmers who make their own cider. Oat-straw is said to impart a good rich colour to the drink; and the dry pomace or "apple-cheese", mixed with it, is excellent food for cattle or pigs, though the former may be easily overfed thereby. By large manu-facturers, and in other districts, hair-cloths are used instead of straw for straining the pomace or "must".

It need hardly be added that there are many varieties of cider-presses, as of cider-mills; some being all of wood and turned by the direct action of levers or crowbars, others being more elaborate contrivances with powerful iron screws and guides and operated by means of a geared windlass.

In South Devon, when the cider has been made, a

little of it used to be poured round the roots of the apple-
tree; a libation perhaps to Pomona or the local deity who
took her place.

HOPS

"At hop-picking they was all home pickers, none of
your London folks. My mother would reckon to get the
money for the children's clothes in the winter. It was all
right when it was fine, but when it was wet the bine of
the hops would tear your hands something cruel. And
then you could never eat enough, it made you so hungry.
The best of it was when the old man came round with
his flat basket of ginger-bread and cakes, and us children
would get a penn'orth. You don't reckon the hardships
then!"

Hops used always to be grown on poles; the use of
strings came in about forty-five years ago. There were
three poles, or occasionally five, to each hill; these were
fixed aslant into the ground and the hops were detached
at harvest-time with a hop-dog—a long-handled implement with a knife at the end and a curled piece, which cut
the bine at the root and pushed it up the stick and off the
top end so that the hops could be picked. The same name
was given in some parts of Kent to a lever for pulling up
the poles. This way of growing hops is no longer so
common, save when new vines are planted: the poles are
now put in to last for fifteen or twenty years and those
near the edge of the field are strengthened with extra
supports. In March men go round the hop-gardens on
stilts tying the strings (there are several systems of
stringing); and in May when the young shoots are about
a foot long they are started round the string in an anti-
clockwise direction, the bine being tied to the poles or
strings with watered rushes. There are very many other
things to do: trench-ploughing or digging between the

rows of hills, hoeing, harrowing, hilling, manuring, spraying and if necessary protecting the sides of the hop-ground from the wind with mats of hop-bine; and the proper tools are required: specially fitted ploughs, hop-ridgets and becks, kufs, spanes and spuds, as the special kinds of hoes, spades and forks are called.

The picking, as everyone knows, brings crowds of Londoners and other townspeople into the country, though fewer now than in former years, for hop-growing has much declined; and no wonder, seeing that nowadays but one pound of hops goes to twenty gallons of beer, not to mention the vast quantities of Bavarian hops which some of our brewers import. The pickers often work in families and the work done by each family used always to be checked by double-tallies, two pieces of wood which fit together and are notched across by the foreman once for each bushel picked; he keeps the longer part, or "tally", while the picker keeps the "check". The hops are picked into wooden frames covered with canvas, called bins or cribs; then after being measured they are carried in great sacks, called pokes, to be dried in the oast-house.

There is much variety in the design of oast-houses, but they are all to be recognised by the sight of their white-boarded conical cowls, with a long projecting vane to keep the opening to leeward: all or nearly all, for a new system of drying has been lately invented by means of a forced draught of hot air, which dries the hops quicker and does not require the old-fashioned cowl, and so in time these may gradually disappear. In Hereford the cowls are pointed at the top and rather different from the Kentish ones, which incline to be wider and flat-topped. It is no uncommon thing for a cowl to be twelve feet high or even more, though seen from the ground this would appear incredible. The vanes are often toothed or waved, or end in a distinctive shape, or have emblems such as loaves, balls or rearing horses on their upper edges, to mark the owner or builder. They turn on vertical spindles, which bear upon a horizontal beam some way down the chimney. These chimneys in the old hop-kilns are of rafters, lath and plaster, hung with tiles; in the new ones of slate or asbestos; and in those of intermediate age they are often of brick, cemented over, and built in courses of decreasing width like the top of a well, very curious to look up into from within.

About four feet below the level where the slope of the chimney begins there is a platform of two-inch battens laid two inches apart; they are covered with horse-hair mats and upon these the hops are spread about six inches deep. On the ground floor below is a brazier, burning charcoal and sulphur or, in most Kentish oasts, charcoal and anthracite, though in Hereford they use Welsh coal alone. There are very many possible arrangements for the fire, but it can always be regulated by a shutter to exclude or admit the air. Two driers live and sleep in the oast-house for the fortnight or so in which the work is going on; and once in every few hours they go upstairs and turn the hops with barn-shovels. This generally means going outside and climbing some steps, for to avoid draughts there are no inner stairs. After twelve hours (though sometimes longer) the hops are dry; a double handful of them can be gathered up and pressed closely in a ball, when they will gradually expand and separate again like a silk handkerchief. They are swept out of the chimney on to the upper floor of the oast-house, to lie in heaps for a few days, and thence to a hole from which hangs a pocket or bag eight feet long, its mouth hooked over an iron ring. Into this they are pressed, part at a time, generally with a ram or plunger worked by a winch. Counterpoised presses are now made to lighten this work but it is possible that on one or two very small farms the old way of treading them in may still survive. One of the driers, the "bagster", used to get into the sack, keeping up a song all the time as he turned round and round in it stamping or dancing on the hops, which the "feeder" shovelled in down his back. He wore flat shoes and a round hat of thick plaited straw, nearly as big round as the mouth of the sack, to prevent the hops from flying out again.

At the end of the picking the workers would have a tea and a "frolic" in the barn.

MALTING

The practice of malting is now almost entirely in the hands of large firms of brewers, who have, it is hardly necessary to say, substituted machinery and large-scale production for the old laborious handling so far as the nature of barley allows them. But there used to be in many towns and large villages in barley-growing districts an almost incredible number of malthouses; in the small town of Marshfield, for instance, there are said to have been eighty within living memory. Maltsters belonged to the class of skilled agricultural labourers rather than to that of mechanics, and their work was so important to farmers and the country generally that I shall briefly describe the old method, the survival of which is indeed something of a rarity. Mr Bevan, the landlord of the "George and Dragon", Batheaston, whose family were once great barley-growers, is one of the few innkeepers who still brew their own beer; he also employs a maltster. Before the barley is ready for malting it must generally be "sweated" in kilns, sometimes for five or six weeks. After this it is put in water, in which the heavier grains sink and the lighter ones float. The latter are skimmed off, as being useless for malting, and these skimmings are dried and sent to the miller to grind into barley-meal for poultry or pigs. The sound grains are left in water for fifteen days, then taken out and spread on the floor of the kiln, which was made of flat bricks or tiles, perforated with very small holes. The fire below was of charcoal and the space round and above it was enclosed with a funnel-shaped chimney of metal, increasing to the size of the floor. On this floor the grains were turned over with a broad wooden shovel once every twelve hours and sprinkled with water between every turning. Soon they would begin to sprout and after the third turning, when the sprouts were about a quarter of an inch long, the fire was made up and the malt heated for a day, until it was completely dry.

The tendency as soon as the grains begin to sprout is for them to become matted together so that they cannot be separated, and to prevent damage from this cause the "floor of malt" was ploughed through, up and down in straight lines, by the maltster who pushed along a three-pronged pike (the "barley-fork" illustrated)—an operation known as furling. After this the malt was collected in bags and ground. The maltster also put out the fire and descended into the funnel-shaped chimney below the floor, from which he carefully collected all the malt-dust which had fallen through the perforations in the bricks.

Barley-fork
(Marshfield, Glos)

Chapter XIV

FLAX

FLAX is grown in England near Selby, Yorkshire, and in the neighbourhood of Yeovil; in both places its cultivation was revived by the Government during the war. Sixty or seventy years ago flax was a flourishing industry in Somerset—in the village of Chisel-borough alone there were a dozen flax shops—but the trade was killed by Russian imports, when steamers became common and freights cheaper. So the traditional way of dressing flax is no more than a memory; for the modern method is a good deal different in many details and involves the use of more complicated machinery. The part of the flax plant from which linen thread is made is the outer skin or fibres of the stem; and the seed (linseed) is most valuable for oil and for cattle food.

Flax is sown broadcast in April, the stems growing up close together some three feet high. They bear small round flowers of a beautiful azure blue, which, though they fade in the sunlight, close up in the evening and the next morning come out as blue as ever. When these have fallen and the seed-vessels have formed, in late July, it is time to pull the flax. The flax-gatherers work across the field, following one another, so that the pulling is done in steps, like mowing or reaping. They pull it up swiftly by the roots, using each hand alternately, and throw it out in swaths as they go. It may lie there for a day or two till it is somewhat dry, when it is gathered up by a man working down the swath and collecting the sheaves between his bent body and thighs. He then ties it, as all sheaves and bundles should be tied, with its "own bond".

When the seed vessels are dry enough the seed must

be stamped out, and for this a stamping-bill was used. The head of the stamping-bill was made of the curved outer slice of an elm log, about ten inches long by eight wide, the under face being flat or with slight ridges. The handle is a stout but slightly flexible ash-staff four or five feet long, set obliquely into the head. With this the seed is beaten out, the flax being laid on the ground under cover.

The flax is then tied up loosely in bundles and spread thinly over the ground by women and children for "dew-retting", that is to allow the inner part of the stem (the "skimps") to rot and the gum which holds them to the outer fibres to decompose. These bundles are turned over with sticks occasionally, so that both sides may be equally retted. The rotting flax has a very strong, rather unpleasant smell, like old corduroy breeches in the rain. The retting may take six days or six weeks, according to the dews and rains; when stems begin to crack and open—this was called "grinning"—it is a sign that the retting has gone far enough. The bundles are now cocked up to dry, the seed end upwards and the roots spread round in a circle, the cocks having a slight twist to keep them together; and when they are dry enough to be tied up without danger of rotting at the bonds, they are tied again in bundles and made into ricks.

In the old process, before it was to be worked, the flax was spread out on a sort of platform of long poles, built against a wall and raised some three feet from the ground, and a smouldering fire made of "skimps" beneath it. This was sometimes stirred by a man with a stick, who must take care that there was heat enough to dry the flax without risk of setting fire to it, for it would all blaze up in a moment. The dried flax was carried in the evening to the haling-house and kept warm till next day, when it was to be scutched and swingled. The haling-house was a domed brick oven, in which a fire was made till all the bricks were well warmed. The ashes were carefully raked out and every spark extinguished; then the flax was taken in and covered up with sacks. Next morning it was "crips and crappy" (crisp and crackling) and not tough as it would have been if left uncovered overnight.

For scutching, the oldest kind of brake was a hinged framework of long wooden bars, triangular in section, which fitted together, top and bottom, when the frame was shut. The flax was pressed between these to "frack up" the skimps, or inner part, which must be got rid of. Later serrated rollers were invented, to be turned by hand like a mangle; and the modern machine, though mechanically driven, is on the same principle.

The swingle was like a wooden hatchet with a curved bill projecting in front. Each flax dresser stood before his flax-board—a tapered plank, round-ended and thin, the top coming to hand-height and the bottom fixed slantwise to a stump in the ground—held the flax in his left hand with the heads across the end of his board, and clipped the stems with his swingle to beat out the skimps. He used the curved end of the swingle to knock the stems into place again on the board. The seedy ends of the flax he combed out on a comb fixed to the wall; these combings are tow.

The swingled flax was preferred in a "ribbony" rather than a "woolly" state. It did not matter if a few of the "tags" (roots) were left at the ends of the fibres; this was better than cutting them off too short. Two six-pound bundles were tied together at the ends to make a "head"; the ends were brought to a tapering "whip-top" and laced together for six or eight inches down. Flax is still tied up in twelve-pound heads, but the old custom of lacing it up is no longer practised, though there are some living who can do it; it was merely a graceful finish belonging to a time when work-folk made the most of their jobs.

Formerly flax-dressing was a seasonal occupation, carried on in the winter only, but now it is done all the year round, the whole crop being stored together and drawn from as required.

A good flax crop may amount to three packs an acre, the pack consisting of twenty dozen heads. It seems not to exhaust the land so much as is sometimes supposed, but because it grows so thickly it cannot be hoed or otherwise weeded, and so in a wet year it will leave the ground very foul, though in a dry year, beyond a little bacon-weed, no harm will be done.

Flax was grown by Mr Lenthall at Burton Bradstock, near Bridport, Dorset, up till 1914. It was prepared in the traditional West of England manner, in all respects as at Bradford Abbas, save that the haling-house, instead of being a brick oven, was a timber-framed shed with thatched sides and roof, in which the flax after drying was merely covered up with sacks to keep warm overnight. The stamping-bills were made by Mr Lenthall's father; they had elm heads and flexible handles of withy-wood, plugged into their sockets with tow. In Yorkshire flax, or line as it is called by the farmers there, has for many years been collected from the farms, where it is grown and pulled, and taken to the factory to be prepared, so the traditional way of treating it there is hardly remembered. But the industry is in a bad way now, for the same reason that has been fatal to so many of the best traditions in British agriculture; the public demand is for cheap inferior foreign stuff, instead of more expensive, but sound and lasting goods.

TEAZLE

Teazles are used for dressing cloth, the heads being fixed in a revolving frame or gig-mill, which combs the cloth and raises the nap of the wool. Artificial substitutes made of wire have been devised in Germany, but teazles are still superior, so that the best cloth is still dressed with them. Crops of teazle were formerly grown in most parts of Somerset, and they are still cultivated near Ilminster, at Curry Mallet, Curry Rivel and Hatch Beauchamp, and also, it is said, near Halifax and Huddersfield. But the crop is an uncertain one and its value extremely variable.

Teazle grows best on a light soil with a clay subsoil to hold its roots; lacking such anchorage the plant may easily be blown down by the wind. It takes two years to reach maturity, when it may be as much as seven feet high and bear from forty to a hundred heads. The terminal heads which grow upon upright stems, one in the middle of each plant and longer than any of the other stems, are called "kings". These are the largest and finest; the others may be of second or third quality, called middlings and scrubs, or else owing to some fault of growth or shape may even be rejected altogether. In the cultivated teazle the hooked points of the head turn down and are firmer and of a cleaner and less clinging shape than in the wild teazle, which would be useless for the purpose.

It is sown in April or early May; and the plants when just coming up look somewhat like lettuces. In October they are replanted with more space. The leaves grow in pairs, and each pair of leaves forms a cup round the stem which holds water to nourish the plant. The following July it flowers, the blossoms appearing in a clustered ring halfway up the head and spreading upwards and downwards, so that those in the middle have fallen before the ends have flowered. In late July or August it must be cut. The leaves and stems are very thorny, so that thick gloves must be worn by the cutters, who with a short curved knife gather them in handfuls (of as many as thirty heads, if small) with stems about eight inches long, tying each bundle with a bond made from the stem of a "king"; and to be more easily carried the bundles are fastened to poles. They are dried in the sun and stored till November, when dealers from Leeds or Huddersfield come round to buy them.

A pack of teazles contains 20,000 heads and may be worth anything from £20 (as it was after the war, when the French were not allowed to grow any teazles) to only £5 according to the crop and the quantity grown. Now they are generally packed in bags which will hold 10,000 of the largest size; but formerly the bundles were very prettily arranged on sticks and so loaded up into the carts which took them away.

The same ground must not be sown with teazles for seven years.

OTHER LOCAL AND OCCASIONAL CROPS

There is not much purpose in attempting here to describe at length the cultivation and treatment of other crops which were once a source of wealth to British farmers, but are no longer grown. Hemp was at one time an important product of Norfolk and Lincolnshire, but even the oldest labourers do not now remember it. Liquorice was also grown as a crop in Lincolnshire (it was last grown in Tilney in 1927) and many people will recollect buying the native root, in penny chunks or slivers, at the town markets and chemists' shops, as a sovereign cure for winter coughs; it was a thing entirely different in nature from the repulsive black "bootlace" so eagerly devoured by modern urchins or the thick unpleasant mass of liquorice powder and water. Lemon balm, and other spices for flavouring, have also been grown lately, but on a very small scale. Saffron is still used a great deal in Cornwall, but it is all imported from France.

The last English woad-farm to survive (at Boston, Lincolnshire) planted none in 1931, the reason being, it seems, that not enough people in the country care enough about wearing clothes of a fine blue colour, which will stand for five years instead of two, to pay a single farmer's expenses in cultivating and preparing the crop; notwithstanding that it was used in policemen's uniforms. The other dyer's plants, weld (which gives a yellow pigment) and madder (which gives crimson) have for long gone out of cultivation in this country, though there are no doubt some Dutch farmers who can still make the latter pay.

The very interesting details of the history and culture of woad (pronounced "wod" in Lincolnshire) and the after-processes of crushing, balling, drying, grinding, couching and barrelling, are not related here, for they form the subject of a book recently published by the late Dr J. B. Hurry. It may, however, be worth recording that the woadman, in sending off the barrels of woad, would cry after the waggon "Speed her well!" an ancient custom, doubtless, which has died only with the trade.

Teazle knife (Brent Knoll, Somerset)

Chapter XV

TURF-CUTTING: EXMOOR

PEAT-TURF is cut in late May and early June, on Exmoor, Sedgemoor and other places in Somerset. It is used locally for fuel and some is sent away for this and for other purposes, but not half as much is now cut as in former years. On Exmoor there are several kinds: "spine-turf", which grows on the shale and is only a couple of inches thick, and bog-peat, which may go down to a depth of many feet and is blacker and more valuable for fuel the deeper it is found. Heather and other plants turn into peat as they decompose and more vegetation grows upon them. In spine-turf the most important element is a kind of grass called "ciphers", which grows in little knots or tufts.

To cut spine-turf the old method is for a man called the "cutter" to drive a breast-plough into it, by leaning on the cross-handle with the thighs, while another person, generally a woman, called the "stretcher", lifts up the corner and eases it as the blade of the plough is worked under. Though varying in size, the turves are generally about three feet long by one foot wide; and they are cut out here and there, wherever the surface looks promising. On Winsford-hill all the turf may not be ploughed off, but strips must be left between, so that the "spine" may grow across again and form new turf. Here a breast-plough is used with a blade of another shape.

The deeper turf is cut downwards in "spits" with Scotch spades; the turves are smaller and regular in shape. Once cut and dried, the turf must not be wet again, especially if it be spine-turf. This should dry hard and stiff and break like a biscuit; and if the rain has been on it it cannot so easily be dried again—it remains limp, and burns much less well. The broken turf gathered up after rain is called "briss".

If rain threatens when the turf is drying, it must be gathered up into "burroughs", or "burroughed up", each heap containing about 250 turves. As soon as it is dry it is carried and stored under cover. Formerly it was carried on "slides", small sledges without wheels and sometimes with a curved stick at either side as a rail, but now flat Exmoor carts are used, like Scotch carts, with railed sides. Slides, which were also used in harvesting hay on the hills, are nearly extinct here, though in North Wales and other mountainous districts they are very commonly used.

CHARCOAL-BURNING

Charcoal is still used to some extent as fuel in the Kentish oast-houses, though anthracite has largely taken its place; and it was used for malting also. The charcoal-burner's has now become a rare enough calling to justify a short account here.

The whole process takes about a week, but the charcoal-burner will often keep two fires going at once. The space on which they stand is sheltered from the wind by hedges and generally also by thatched hurdles or "looes", which can be moved round as the wind changes and are held upright by poles. Each fire is about twenty feet across and consists of cord-wood, that is stout sticks or slender stakes, four feet long. A cord of wood is a rectangular heap of it made between upright stakes, four feet broad, four high and eight long. Some straw or brushwood is placed in the middle and the wood heaped round it on end, the first lengths being stood on end and the outer ones being gradually sloped inwards. When enough have been laid, the whole heap is covered with straw or heather over which earth or ashes are shovelled, sprinkled with water, and beaten down with the flat of the shovel till there are no gaps left. Then the fire is lighted in the centre, often with the hot ashes from the last fire, and the centre also covered with damped cinders. Finally a few holes are made round the top to act as just sufficient vents.

The charcoal-burner lives in a hut close to the fire, for every few hours he must attend to it, throwing buckets of water on the ashes and flattening them down with his shovel, watching every change of wind in case the wood should begin to burn, for it must only smoulder and as much as possible of the heat must be kept in and not allowed to escape. He knows exactly when the charcoal is all ready and then begins carefully raking off the ashes with which it is covered. He breaks it into lumps two or three inches long, packs them into bags, which are stored away in a dry shelter, and carefully sweeps out the circle in readiness for the next fire.

Owing to the nature of his work which, unless he has a wife or assistant, occupies him more or less constantly as long as the charcoal-burning season lasts (which is generally from about August to November), the charcoal-burner is a specialist at any rate during that season. For the rest of the year he may help to work a steam-engine for threshing or do a bit of hedge-cutting or carting, but the next year he reappears at the same spot, his face and hands still ingrained with charcoal-dust and his clothes plastered with it till their folds are as rigid and uniform as the creases in the hide of a rhinoceros.

Chapter XVI

MOLE-CATCHING

THE question whether moles ought to be killed has been occasionally disputed, but farmers generally reckon that the harm they do in throwing up earth over the grass and making it uneven outweighs their usefulness as cultivators of the soil and devourers of worms and grubs. Nothing more quickly blunts the edge of a scythe or grass-cutting machine than to be driven into earth, especially if it contain pebbles or grit. Gervase Markham treats of moles at length; and his statement of the case for and against them is still typical of some rustic debates: "...howsoever some Husbandmen say, moe Moale-hills more ground; yet tis certaine, that moe Moale-hills, less good ground for never yet was sweet grasse seene on a Moale-hill".

Markham mentions several substances whose scent is objectionable to moles—chopped onions, Palma Christi, and burning sulphur—and also these three ways of killing them:

"1st. Moale-spearing (to open a burrow and wait with a spear).

2nd. Flooding the land with water.

3rd. The last (indeed as much approued as any) is to take a liue Moale in the moneth of March, which is their bucking or ingendring time, and put it into a deepe brasse Bason, or other deepe smooth Vessell, out of which the imprisoned Moale cannot creepe, and then at evening bury it in the earth up to the brimme, and so leave it, and the imprisoned Moale will presently beginne to shrike, or complaine or call, so that all the Moales in the ground will come to it, and tumbling into the Vessell, they are prisoners also, and the more prisoners the greater will bee the noise; and the more noise, the more Moales will come to the rescue, so that I haue seene 50 or 60 taken in one night, and in one vessell or brasse Kettle.''

Some use dogs to catch moles, others shoot them as they see them heaving the ground; often the spud is used to fling them out of their tunnels, but to succeed with this you must put your heel in the tunnel far enough behind the mole. These are the modern equivalents of mole-spearing, a practice which doubtless went out when powder and shot came in. Some old farmers used to burn brown-paper candles, dipped in brimstone, in the runs. Smoke-cartridges have been fired to suffocate the moles, but these are said to be of little avail, as there is a lower set of workings into which the little creatures quickly betake themselves. It would be hard to conceive of a farmer flooding his pastures in order to drown the moles; and notwithstanding the spectacular results described by Markham, the third method also seems to have passed into oblivion. An old mole-catcher in Hereford, however, described a trap by which he had caught a number of moles together; this was a large box, buried in the run, with a trap-fall in the lid which turned over with the weight of each mole that went along that way.

When the now elderly generation of labourers has passed, but few of the many old-fashioned traps and baits will be remembered; and perhaps it is no harm that they should be forgotten, for some were cruel and few so instantly effective as the steel spring-traps which are now used nearly everywhere. There is also a patent poison, to sprinkle on earthworms, which form the chief food of moles. This is not a new idea, for at least a century ago nux vomica and chopped earthworms were mixed and laid on the ground. By this means the moles are lost; moreover, moles skin their prey before they eat it, and so may rid the bait of its poison.

There are a good many professional mole-catchers in the eastern counties; they are regularly employed by the Fen Draining Boards in Cambridgeshire, on account of the damage which moles do by tunnelling the banks of the canals or drains. These men work in the winter only, when moleskin is at its best, and they use traps of their own making. The trap is set in the main passage which leads from the moles' hunting-ground to their permanent quarters. The moles pass up this at about nine in the morning and return about ten in the evening; and mole-catchers say that it is of no use to set traps after midday. To set the trap a section is dug cleanly out of the roof of the tunnel with the spud, of just sufficient length to take the trap. The mole-catcher's spud is a tool with a square cutting iron point and a handle of about the right height to walk with; for very stiff ground he has another one with a longer blade and socket. The trap consists of a board with a small hole in the middle and a narrow hoop at either end. Two nooses of thin copper wire are pressed round inside the hoops, and their ends are drawn through the board and fastened to a cord of which one end is tied to the top of a hazel switch. This switch is bent down to the ground by means of a shorter cord, which is held in the hole in the board by a small wooden peg, which projects downwards from the board into the tunnel, between the two nooses. The board is firmly pegged down to the ground with a couple of forked willow-shoots. When the mole pushes against the peg and loosens it, the cord is released and the hazel rod springs up, tightening the noose round the mole's body. In parts of Norfolk a more primitive form is made, with wooden hoops and a forked peg.

Some of the old traps in Somersetshire consisted of a heavy square block of wood which on being released fell on to a socket and crushed the mole. A snare which many countrymen know how to set is made simply of a horsehair or wire noose laid in the run and fastened to a switch, of which the end is bowed over and notched under a peg. The mole puts his head through the noose and agitates it, the nicked end is disengaged, the switch flies up straight and the mole is hanged. This snare is also laid for rats. Another trap, used on the pastures in Romney Marsh, had a small wooden barrel made to fill the run; it was no bigger than a quarter-pound cocoa-tin and it had in either end a leather sleeve or valve, which was well rubbed with earth. This was carefully covered with grass and earth and attached to a hazel switch sprung under a peg as in the other traps, so that the agitation caused by the mole in it would suffice to spring the trap, and the creature would be suspended alive in the barrel.

Moles are cannibals, and it is said that they cannot go without food for more than four hours. If several of them are shut up together for a night, in the morning one of them will have been eaten clean to the skeleton. Everyone who has tried to catch them must know that, though feeble of sight, moles are very sensitive to light and will avoid a trap where the least chink of daylight is left to show. Moreover, they are quick of hearing and very keen of scent, and therefore the mole-catcher must rub his hands with earth and not allow any smell of tobacco or beer to enter the burrow.

In most places, however, there is no longer scope for the countryman's art in making traps nor for such great skill in setting them, for spring-traps and poison are much easier to use; nor, through fashion's vagaries, is there now much demand for moleskin, though it is the closest, softest and warmest of furs and will lie smoothly in any direction.

"The Monkey-jumper" (Church Farm, Newchurch, Kent)

Breast-plough (Mr William Ball, Ashwick, Gloucestershire)

Reaping oats, near Glenbeigh, Co. Kerry

Drawing reed for thatching (Higher Pymore, near Bridport, Dorset)

The Bamlett "Sailer" (Lutton Bank, Lincs)

Threshing (Tyllwydd, near Llanbister)

Straw ornaments

Harvest festival ricks (Stoke, near Rochester)

Straw doll hung in porch of Over-
bury Church, near Tewkesbury

For EU product safety concerns, contact us at Calle de José Abascal, 56–1°,
28003 Madrid, Spain or eugpsr@cambridge.org.

www.ingramcontent.com/pod-product-compliance
Ingram Content Group UK Ltd.
Pitfield, Milton Keynes, MK11 3LW, UK
UKHW042212180425
457623UK00011B/185